Managing the Small
Law Enforcement Agency

by the
International Association
of Chiefs of Police

KENDALL/HUNT PUBLISHING COMPANY
2460 Kerper Boulevard P.O. Box 539 Dubuque, Iowa 52004-0539

To order additional copies of this book, call Kendall/Hunt Publishing at
1-800-228-0810

Printed in the United States of America
10 9 8 7 6 5 4 3 2 1

Table of Contents

Preface

The majority of all police departments in the United States are staffed by 25 or fewer sworn officers.

The small agency chief has to balance the resources of his department—manpower and finances—with the concerns and demands of the community in which he works and in many instances, resides. Often his responses must be innovative and creative to stretch available resources and address community issues.

Police chiefs in small towns are a part of the local culture and community. Crime prevention, police community relations, and non-enforcement duties as well as addressing law enforcement matters, are a part of the small department's every day responsibilities. Proactive policing with significant community involvement is an expectation for small town departments. Small town chiefs employ personalized methods of policing and are closer to the community and political powers.

In publishing this book, *Managing the Small Law Enforcement Agency*, the International Association of Chiefs of Police is providing the small agency chief with a practical reference work containing current information and proposed solutions to management issues within the small police organization.

Recognized authorities in the police profession have contributed material to this book which provides the latest thoughts on topical areas of interest to small police agency chief executives. The collective experience of these authorities as presented in *Managing the Small Law Enforcement Agency* will be of significant value to the police executive.

The recent census revealed that for the first time in 60 years, the population growth rate was higher in rural and small town communities in the United States than in metropolitan areas. Even before the census data was released, economists and real estate observers had noted the population migration out of the big cities and into the countryside. Rising crime rates and increasing population mean that the chemistry of the rural or small town community will change. This in turn will mean that the rural or small town police agency must change. This book will help the small agency chief to meet the challenges and changes that the future holds.

INTERNATIONAL ASSOCIATION OF CHIEFS OF POLICE

IACP POLICE

SINCE 1893

The International Association of Chiefs of Police is a professional organization comprised of over 13,000 top law enforcement executives from the United States and over 70 foreign nations. IACP members lead and manage several hundred thousand law enforcement officers and civilian employees in local, state, federal and international law enforcement agencies. Agency heads, from the smallest agency to the largest, meet together to further the goals of law enforcement.

The leaders of the IACP include many distinquished names in American law enforcement, both past and present. August Vollmer, an early progressive leader in the field was also a president of IACP.

Since 1893, the IACP has facilitated the exchange of important information among police administrators and promoted the highest possible standards of performance and conduct within the police profession. This work is carried out by functionally oriented committees consisting of police practitioners with a high degree of expertise that provide contemporary information on trends, issues, and experiences in policing for development of cooperative strategies, new and innovative programs, and positions for adoption through resolution by the association. Throughout its existence, the IACP has been devoted to the cause of crime prevention and the fair and impartial enforcement of laws with respect for constitutional and fundamental human rights.

To be successful, the modern law enforcement executive needs the latest, most up-to-date information and state-of-the-art equipment. Today's chief must remain alert to new trends and developments that will affect the efficiency and effectiveness of the police department. The police executive must always be poised on the edge of tomorrow, ready to cope with the future.

As the world's leading association of police executives, the IACP has developed a similar posture. The IACP today is organized to deliver the kinds of services needed by modern law enforcement professionals. The assistance we offer to the law enforcement community is both direct and indirect. The vast array of IACP programs, studies, publications, training and networking opportunities contribute in many ways to more efficent and effective law enforcement.

The IACP is ready for tomorrow, willing and able to represent the interests of law enforcement professionals in the challenges that lie ahead.

Chapter 1
Administering a "Micro"
Law Enforcement Agency[1]

The word "small" is a relative term. Certainly, Chicago is a large city, and its police department, with over 12,000 sworn members, is a large department. However, depending upon the size of the organization with which it is being compared, the Chicago police force—large as it is—may be seen as only a moderate-sized group. In the police world, the term "small" has come to mean a department of 15-30 sworn members, which tends to relegate the agencies of 10 or fewer officers to the "miniscule" range, seemingly not worthy of consideration. These "micro" departments comprise 53% of the United States law enforcement agencies and 79% have fewer than 25 sworn officers, according to the Bureau of Justice Statistics, U.S. Department of Justice.

If the advancement of law enforcement is to continue, then *all* law enforcement organizations must be improved. To neglect the small law enforcement agency is to care for the exposed portion of a plant while neglecting the roots. Small law enforcement organizations form the backbone of law enforcement and in the end will be the yardstick against which our efforts toward professionalization will be measured.

The Micro Chief

Regardless of the size of the agency, there is a common thread of responsibility—administrators must provide the most efficient, cost-effective, fair and objective service possible to the people of their respective jurisdictions. From the largest departments to the smallest, police chiefs strive to achieve the same professional service.

1

Just as administrators are learning that today's officers are a "new, better-educated breed," the micro chief is also a new breed. The micro chief is asking questions about the current status of law enforcement and the environment in which he is expected to provide services. While the work of the administrators of any size agency is similar in many respects, the micro chief must often be a "jack of all trades." This results in compromise and juggling of duties to the detriment of the operation as a whole.

The micro chief is an integral part of a jurisdiction's government; in fact, he may be a stranger's first contact with the policy-making arm of the city government. Further, the citizens of a small geographical area expect to have personal contact with the "chief," who more than likely will know many of them on a first-name basis. It follows then, that even the smallest of problems will come to the attention of the micro chief.

While this allows for a more personal application of the criminal justice system, it does place additional constraints on the chief's time. The micro chief must accomplish his administrative duties in between fixing spotlights on squad cars, working a standard shift, typing his own correspondence, going to court or any one of a number of other time-consuming duties.

Concerns of the Micro Agency

The concerns facing the micro agency are probably not much different from the problems confronting any other law enforcement agency; they are only more acute. The main concern centers on the lack of finances. Related problems are manpower, procurement and retention of good officers, training at all levels, specialization, relationships with other organizations and public perception.

Written policy is a duty common to both the micro chief and the chief of a large department. With the increasing number of internal as well as external lawsuits, the development of written policy for the protection of the department, city, officer and chief executive is far too important to be slighted. Lawsuits have no respect for agency size, geographical location or any other factor. In most cases, it is as time-consuming to develop a written policy for a department of eight as for a department of 10,000.

Finances

This is a complex area, controlled by many outside influences. The economic situation in a particular area and the attitudes of its citizens—specifically the governing body—are very crucial factors. Of course, there are a few "well-heeled" micro agencies in the nation, but these are the exception, not the rule. Generally, micro departments must operate on less money per employee—for salary, benefits, equipment, office space, uniforms, etc.—than do large agencies.

Manpower

Financial limitations also have an effect on the manpower available to the micro chief. Many departments cannot adequately staff shifts based upon needs and calls for services.

An associated problem lies with the procurement and retention of qualified personnel. With the drive toward professionalism, police salaries in many areas have risen to a level commensurate with the services required. Unfortunately, however, in many areas micro departments have not been able to keep pace. The starting salary for a patrol officer in one micro jurisdiction is $9,000 less than at a larger agency only 35 miles away. The pool of applicants from which the micro department must choose is, of course, adversely affected.

Yet to hire a recruit without police experience is not usually practical because of the lengthy training process required. Basic training alone for a new recruit represents a substantial investment. This does not include salary, field training programs, uniforms and equipment. This can become a burden *extraordinaire* for the micro department. As a result, the micro agency, which is least able to afford it, becomes a training school and is forced to adjust its manpower qualifications to keep a full staff.

These limitations make it necessary for many micro departments to attract personnel on other basis. Simply because hiring a certified officer allows them to have a man on the street in a relatively short amount of time, some agencies are tempted to "buy" a larger department's personnel problem. Other agencies have experienced difficulty in retaining highly qualified persons because their eyes will generally be on a higher-paying department. The use of the micro department as a stop-gap measure by such officers causes severe budget problems for that agency.

Long-range planning of a training program is also extremely difficult. If an officer is designated to attend training away from the department, it only takes one other officer to quit the force or get sick or injured to throw the proverbial monkey wrench into the plans.

Micro agencies have no more immunity from lawsuits that claim improper or insufficient training than an agency of any other size, yet the micro chief is literally forced to adjust manpower qualifications to staff the department.

Specialization

The need for even minimal specialization was recognized as far back as 1967 by the President's Commission on Law Enforcement and the Administration of Justice, which stated: "If progress is to be realized in achieving professional stature, there must be a separating out of the functions so that those of a purely ministerial nature are performed by persons of lesser talents, receiving compensation commensurate with the job."

The manpower and mobilization problems make any specialization of the investigative process difficult, if not impossible, for many agencies. A proper criminal investigation takes the same form and is as important to quality work regardless of the size of the community. In order to provide a good criminal investigation, manpower, knowledge and equipment are absolute musts. The micro department must juggle schedules, money and manpower in order to produce that specialized person. However, specialists in the micro department are still required to fill in for other officers on a regular basis.

For example, one Virginia micro chief, recognizing an increase of Part I crimes going uncleared due to the workload and inability of patrol officers to follow up, created an investigator slot in his 12-member police department. Within two months, due to the loss of one man, in-service training requirements and vacations, the investigator was back on the patrol schedule. Long-term investigations, such as arson, armed robbery or burglary are compromised and the micro department, along with the community it has sworn to protect, suffer as the result.

Training

Micro chiefs have been wrongly accused of using lack of resources and knowledge as an excuse for a poorly trained department. Due to manpower limitations, the micro chief must perform the most basic of patrol functions while his officers obtain the training they need. With ever-changing court decisions, technological advancements, procedural changes of other governmental agencies, legislative decisions and normal "brushing up," training is a nonstop process. Obviously, micro departments do not have the resources to take on much in-house training, so most training takes place outside the department despite severe budget constraints.

Public Perception

The micro chief has been and in some instances still is guilty of aggravating an already improperly balanced system. The "Barney Fyfe" image of the micro chief still holds true in too many cases. Sloppiness in dress, report writing, investigations and record-keeping does more to maintain this image than any outside influence ever could. These slovenly habits can sometimes be absorbed and covered in a larger agency, but never in a micro department. The battle against laziness and apathy must be a constant one to avoid carryover into the attitudes of the officers, the citizens of the community and the governing bodies.

The prevailing "Barney Fyfe" image is reflected by television, the public, larger agencies, governing bodies and even the criminal element, but this is no reason for us to accept that image.

Solutions

Micro chiefs need to realize that one of their most important tasks is the education of their employing governing bodies as to the small law enforcement function. Negative citizen attitudes toward finances will change only if the chief asserts himself in a positive, non-threatening manner, and seeks the finances necessary to operate a professional service.

Chiefs of small town police departments need help with public education programs directed toward the small communities regarding the uniqueness in the policing field. They also need the educational and training tools to learn to handle violent crimes (which do occur in micro policing), but these programs must be tailored to their needs and be more accommodating to their less flexible schedules. A mobile training facility attached to a parent organization that would operate with the micro chief on *his* schedule rather than that of the organization should receive proper attention from the state training commission.

Police executive associations need to become more aware of—and responsive to—unique situations and problems in small towns. Granted, this is a two-way street and these associations cannot be responsive unless the small chiefs participate.

Some of the areas of primary concern have been mentioned: the finances and resulting manpower, equipment, training problems and the attitudinal factors facing the micro chief. The key to all of this lies ultimately with the micro chief, but he needs the support and understanding of other law enforcement administrators.

Endnote

[1]From an article written by Robert Brandekamp, Jeanne Heuberger and John Wolford, "A Micro What? Administering a Small Town Police Department," *Police Chief,* November 1983.

Review Questions - Chapter 1

1. In most instances, the main concern the micro agency chief has is:
   a. *training at all levels.*
   b. *public perception of agency.*
   c. *lack of finances.*
   d. *manpower.*

2. "Micro" police departments are described as agencies with 10 or fewer officers and, according to a Bureau of Justice Statistics report, compromise the following approximate percent of this country's law enforcement agencies:
   a. *30 percent*
   b. *75 percent*
   c. *53 percent*
   d. *92 percent*

Chapter 2
Issues in Small Town Policing[1]

Who are the rural and small town police in the United States today? What do they do? How do rural and small town policing differ from suburban and urban policing? Why do they differ?

It has been felt that the rural and small town law enforcement agencies have been overlooked, neglected and frequently ignored even though they account for most of the law enforcement agencies in the United States. Researchers have concentrated on the metropolitan police, and a disproportionately large share of the monies have gone to urban and suburban police departments. The mass media has long discriminated against rural and small town police with stereotypes and prejudices. A few studies have been done about rural crime, but very little is known and less is written about rural and small town police. Rural and small town police remain the great unexplored mystery of the criminal justice system.

Four Variables

If the very limited amount of available data is representative of the entire population of rural and small town police, then four variables—salary, education, training and age—are significantly different between metropolitan and nonmetropolitan police.

Salary. Rural and small town police officers are paid significantly less than their urban counterparts. There is a direct relationship between the size of the police agency and the average annual salary of its individual officers. The larger the agency, the larger the salary; the smaller the agency, the smaller the salary.

Education. There is a direct correlation between the size of the police agency and the average education of its officers. The larger the police agency, the more years of education the average individual officer is likely to have. Perhaps the best explanation for this is the attractive salaries that the larger agencies offer beginning officers and the large number of beginning officers who have just completed some college study and can easily relocate.

Training. The same relationship is found in regard to training. The larger the agency, the more police training the average officer is likely to have had. Smaller police department officers do not receive as much basic academy training by a field training officer, roll-call training, specialized training or in-service training as officers employed by suburban or big city police departments. Limited budgets, resources and manpower seem to be the most frequent explanations for the limited training. Training efforts, like federal monies, go to those who ask and demand. Larger police agencies are more likely to have the sophistication and expertise required to ask and demand.

Age. Police officers employed by rural and small town police departments are older than urban officers. There is a definite negative relationship between the size of the police agency and the average age of its officers. Although there is evidence to indicate this gap between the ages of rural police officers and urban police officers is narrowing, it does still exist. Perhaps turnover rate and tenure of rural and small town police officers account for the older ages.

Community Involvement

Other studies suggest rural and small town police officers are less bureaucratically organized and have less of a career commitment to policing than do suburban and urban officers. Rural and small town police tend to work where they live, while suburban and urban police tend to live where they work. This is the first of several differences that suggest rural and small town police are better integrated into the mainstream of community life than are metropolitan police.

Rural and small town police are closer to their community than are urban police. Rural and small town police are a part of the local culture and community, whereas urban police tend to form a subculture and move apart from the community. Crime prevention, police community relations and nonenforcement duties all depend on the community for success. Proactive policing requires the community involvement rural and small town police have always experienced. It doesn't matter if a police administrator subscribes to the law enforcement model or the social service model of policing, his department will not be effective if there is an appreciable distance between his department and the community. Urban police tend to be efficient; rural police tend to be effective.

Rural and small town police are trusted by members of the community. Many big city residents fear the police. Because of the very complex sociology of metropolitan areas, citizens are often not sure of the role of the police. The rural dweller or small town resident has a much clearer picture of the police role. Likewise, the rural or small town police officer understands his role better and is not so frequently caught between the horns of a dilemma. The urban officer answers to the police department. The rural or small town officer is held accountable for his actions by the community.

Rural and small town police are also closer to political powers than are urban police. Urban police are insulated from both the community and the political powers by the bureaucracy of their department.

Advantages. Being closer to the community has many police advantages for the rural or small town officer. The nonmetropolitan police officer is in a better position to know what situations require investigation. The rural or small town police officer is usually very familiar with not only the people in his jurisdiction, but also the vehicles and places. A strange vehicle parked in a citizen's driveway raises the suspicions of the rural or small town police officer, while the same car in a suburban driveway goes unnoticed by the metropolitan officer. The rural or small town officer feels he is a part of the community. The small town officer quickly responds and chases the cow out of the garden without complaining; he knows that is part of his job. The outer-urban officer knows the juveniles and adults in his community and delivers appropriate, personalized service when necessary.

Critics point to the personalized and informal methods of rural and small town police as unprofessional. Perhaps "professionalizing" them would erode their effectiveness. Maybe metropolitan policing could learn something about police effectiveness from rural and small town police. It is possible that "professionalizing" rural and small town police would destroy the close and effective personal relationships they have long enjoyed with their community and its citizens.

In a big city, a citizen calls the police for help and gets a uniformed law enforcement officer. In a small town a citizen calls the police for help and gets a human they know by face if not by name. In small towns and rural areas, it is not uncommon for a citizen to call for help and ask for a particular officer by name.

Disadvantages. Being closer to the community has some disadvantages for the rural or small town officer. There are several stress factors that are unique to rural and small town police officers. The rural officer frequently handles calls alone that require two or more officers according to standard police techniques. Rural households are often heavily armed and the police officer is aware of this. These two facts—the absence of a backup and the presence of weapons—make for a lonely, stressful situation.

The rural or small town police officer cannot escape his role, and is often viewed by the community as a 24-hour police officer. This generates stress because the officer cannot participate in the social activities of the community as a person but is forced to be constantly identified as a police officer. Additionally, the rural officer often has known the person with whom he is dealing for many years. When an urban officer stops a traffic violator, chances are he has never seen that person before and will never see him again. When a rural or small town officer stops a traffic violator, chances are he has seen that person before and expects to see that person again many times in day-to-day living. These social factors cause stress unique to rural and small town police.

Lower salaries, lack of training and local politics also contribute to stress. Since rural officers are generalists by the very nature of their tasks and working conditions, transferring or becoming specialists are not alternative avenues open to the officer trying to cope. Inactivity contributes to police stress. Although all police suffer periods of inactivity, other variables make inactivity especially stressful for the rural or small town officer. The rural officer develops perceptions of himself as being incompetent because of the mass media and popular stereotypes of both urban and rural police officers. These perceptions, even though false, create stress and affect performance.

Future. What does the future hold for rural and small town police? Review of a recent Uniform Crime Report will reveal crime rates in all categories are increasing faster for rural and small town areas than for the United States as a whole for major metropolitan areas. The rural or small town police officer is no longer concerned only with an occasional property crime. Whether or not his training has adequately prepared him, the rural officer is now concerned with all types of crimes.

The 1980 census revealed that for the first time in 60 years, the population growth rate was higher in rural and small town communities in the United States than in metropolitan areas. Even before the census data was released, economists and real estate observers had noted the population migration out of the big cities and into the countryside. Rising crime rates and an increasing population mean that the chemistry of the rural or small town community will change. This in turn will mean that the rural or small town police agency must change.

Summary

There seems to be a general perception that rural and small town police have less training, education, salary, formality, bureaucratic organization, career commitment, professionalization and efficiency than urban officers. While older, they are very effective, use more personalized methods of policing and are much closer to the community and the political powers than are urban officers. Rural and small town officers are in a better position to know what situations require further investigation and how much investigation is necessary. Nonmetropolitan police, however, suffer from a very unfavorable mass media image and experience crimes, police problems and forms of stress that are unique to them.

Crime rates and population growth rates are increasing faster in nonmetropolitan areas than in metropolitan areas. Little objective, scholarly research has been done into the state-of-the-art of rural and small town police. Ignorance of the rural and small town police world is greater than knowledge of the rural and small town police world.

Change is a hallmark of our society. Policing will continue to feel the need to change. All police should accept the future's demands for change as a personal and fraternal challenge. All police—rural, small town, suburban, urban, municipal, county, state and federal—must plan and work together to improve the future world of policing for everyone. Education, like policing, is a living, dynamic process. Any size of police agency, whether metropolitan or nonmetropolitan, can learn, if it is willing, from another. Learning, like policing, never ends.

Endnote

[1]From an article written by Vic Sims, "Rural and Small Town Police," *Police Chief*, July 1982.

Review Questions - Chapter 2

1. Four variables which are significantly different between large metropolitan and small rural police forces are
   a. *salary, size, training and age.*
   b. *salary, education, training, and age.*
   c. *salary, crime rate, age and retention.*
   d. *salary, size, clearance rate and age.*

2. Perhaps the biggest advantage which the rural police officer has over the urban police officer is
   a. *salary and working conditions.*
   b. *opportunity for advancement.*
   c. *knowledge of his community.*
   d. *career commitment.*
3. In what ways are small town police more involved with and better integrated into their communities?

Chapter 3
Organizational Beliefs and Values[1]

Editor's Note: Although this chapter, written by Chief Lee P. Brown, and published under the title "A Police Department and Its Values," refers to the Houston Police Department, the policing values discussed apply to all police agencies.

Our society is currently undergoing changes that are revolutionary in their magnitude. These changes will affect all our social institutions, thereby creating a new social order with new relationships between citizens and society's institutions. As a result, delivering police services will be more difficult than at any time during the entire history of policing in America.

To be successful during this period of rapid social change, police agencies must define and articulate those beliefs that guide the institution. Such beliefs are best expressed as values from which the police agency can set policy, deliver services and implement programs. A police department's success during these times will depend, in great part, on the extent to which they adhere to their stated values. Furthermore, the department, if it is to meet the challenge of rapid change, must be prepared to alter the manner in which it has traditionally operated. Its value system, set forth in clear statements of beliefs and broad goals, will change slowly as society's limits of tolerance are altered. These values can then serve as the parameters for flexibility in organization, operation and procedures. The value system thus becomes the basis for developing plans for change and strategies for delivering police service.

Values in Policing

A set of values should be developed by all chiefs to guide the operations of the department. These values set forth the philosophy of policing and the commitment made by the department to high standards of policing. These values also reflect citizens' expectations, which are ultimately manifested in the department's administrative policies and procedures. For each new procedure or rule issued by the department, a policy statement is included setting forth the values inherent in the development of that procedure. The values as developed by the Houston Police Department are as follows:

The Houston Police Department will involve the community in all policing activities that directly impact the quality of community life.

The police are public safety professionals who serve as the community's key resource in efforts to deal with problems of crime, safety and disorder control. But the police are not solely responsible for these efforts. The community must share equally with the police the responsibility for developing a safe and orderly environment. To achieve such collaboration and shared responsibility requires that the police department willingly permit the community to have access to decisionmaking, policy formulation and information about police operations.

The Houston Police Department believes that while crime prevention is the primary goal, it should vigorously pursue those who commit serious crimes.

The department's primary focus must be crime prevention. When crimes do occur, the department must react with vigorous law enforcement, as this is an important deterrent to serious crime. While the department is committed to working with the community in crime prevention efforts, when crime does occur the department is committed to move aggressively toward arrest and prosecution of the perpetrator.

The Houston Police Department believes that policing strategies used must preserve and advance democratic values.

As a law enforcement agent in a democratic country, the police officer must be the living expression of the values and potentialities of democracy. Police officers must not only know the most effective techniques for enforcing the law and maintaining order, they must perform their duties in a manner that helps to preserve and extend the precious values of a democratic society. Thus, the police must not only respect but protect the rights of all citizens as guaranteed by the United States Constitution.

The Houston Police Department believes that it must structure service delivery in a way that will reinforce the strengths of the city's neighborhoods.

As new and improved police operations are designed, the department is committed to working toward strengthening the quality of neighborhoods in the city. People live in neighborhoods and identify with very localized areas. Beats, community service programs, crime prevention efforts and related activities will all be directed toward strengthening and improving neighborhood life.

The Houston Police Department believes that the public should have input into the development of policies that directly impact the quality of neighborhood life.

The police cannot effectively deal with the crime problem alone. The Houston Police Department will commit itself to a major effort of working at the neighborhood level to develop strategies to impact crime patterns. However, if the police are to work collaboratively with the community in carrying out crime interception and prevention activities, the community must have input into the development of police operational policies that affect the quality of life in the neighborhood. This cooperative relationship will be based on joint planning, active police officer involvement in neighborhood activities and sharing of responsibility for carrying out crime interception and prevention strategies. As a part of this effort, the Houston Police Department will provide neighborhoods with accurate and meaningful descriptions of the crime problem so residents and businesses can fully understand the nature and extent of the problem. Police agencies must not isolate themselves from the community, nor limit community involvement.

The Houston Police Department is committed to managing its resources in a careful and effective manner.

Managing a police department is very similar to operating a business—with the bottom line being quality service delivery to clients with a minimum of costs. The police department must be managed so that there is a maximum return from the expenditure of each tax dollar appropriated. Issues such as employee productivity, fiscal accountability, planning and resource utilization will be carefully studied and procedurally addressed.

The Houston Police Department will seek the input of employees into matters that impact employee job satisfaction and effectiveness.

Effective management must include the active participation of employees in policy development, procedure and strategy design, and program formulation. The involvement of officers in the design of the

Directed Area Responsibility Team program, a project of neighborhood-oriented policing is an example of how such involvement can pay substantial benefits. Policies that directly affect employee job satisfaction, such as transfer policies, need to be addressed with active input from the employees potentially affected.

The Houston Police Department will maintain the highest levels of integrity and professionalism in all its actions.

The integrity of the department must not be compromised. There can be no question or suspicion among the citizenry regarding department ethics. It is imperative the department maintain the highest levels of integrity and credibility, ensuring that its standards are sufficiently high so there is not even a perception among citizens that questionable practices exist. Professionalism, in this sense, means impeccable integrity and careful protection of all citizens' rights. It also includes the maintenance of equally high levels of accountability from those authorized to enforce the law.

The Houston Police Department will seek to provide stability, continuity and consistency in all of its operations.

Policing cannot be an arbitrary affair. Decisions must be carefully made, based upon planning and research into alternatives and their impacts. Change for its own sake is not acceptable. As police improvement progresses, the department will remain committed to ensuring changes are made only when there is a substantial benefit to be derived from that change. To increase consistency of operations, policies will clearly state the department's position on the issue addressed and provide guidance to officers in carrying out their duties. The department believes it cannot have each individual officer operating under his own policies.

Leadership Role

As part of his leadership role, the police chief has the responsibility for establishing the department's value system. This value system, written as statements of policy, will determine how police services are ultimately delivered on the streets of the city. Values are particularly important because they serve as the basis for the development of rules and procedures, resource allocation decisions and police-community interface. By clearly setting forth the agency's values, the chief of police will find employees have a better sense of why rules and regulations are established. In addition, the community can properly focus its attention on the department's values, rather than on technical operational matters that are difficult to understand or place in perspective. Value statements are the linkage between the selection

16

of effective policing strategies by a police agency and the public's need to understand why those strategies have been selected.

Endnote

[1]Lee P. Brown, "A Police Department and Its Values," *Neighborhood Oriented Policing* (IACP), 1988, p. 72.

Review Questions - Chapter 3

1. Discussion: Why are statements of a police agency's values a significant contribution to achieving the goals of the police agency?

2. Based upon the information presented in this chapter, which values are applicable to your agency?

Chapter 4
Goals and Objectives for Departments

One of the most pressing and challenging duties of the police chief executive is establishing goals and objectives toward which all personnel of the police agency should be directing their efforts. But to achieve goals, agency-wide cooperation is necessary.

The establishment and achievement of goals and of objectives follow such similar paths that the words "goal" and "objective" are often interchanged. Authorities generally agree that goal is a more general term than objective. The following definitions will be used throughout this discussion.

1. Goal—A statement of broad direction, general purpose or intent. A goal is general and timeless and is not concerned with a particular achievement within a specified time period.
2. Objective—A desired accomplishment that can be measured within a given time frame and under specifiable conditions. The attainment of the objective advances the system toward a corresponding goal.

Fundamental to the establishment of all goals and objectives is a perception of the problems encountered or anticipated by the agency. Clear definition and careful analysis of the factors generating the problem may clearly indicate possible solutions and suggest appropriate goals and objectives. On the other hand, the failure to perceive or to understand a problem may lead to the establishment of goals or objectives that could be nonproductive or even counterproductive.

Workable Goals and Objectives

Every police agency requires both long- and short-range goals and objectives. Many problems that the police agency wishes to solve may require years of effort, while others lend themselves to a more rapid solution. The more time required for solution of a problem, the less reliable will predictions tend to be. Long-range goals must be more flexible and more adaptable to possible changing conditions than short-range goals, although the latter, too, must be sufficiently flexible to meet changing conditions.

In establishing goals and objectives, the police chief executive is bound, of course, by constitutional limitations and by the laws under which he serves. Additionally, he must insure that the goals and objectives of the agency are consistent with the role of the police.

All goals and objectives should be directly responsive to community needs. Normally, if problem definition and analysis have been adequate and alternative solutions carefully screened, responsiveness to community needs can be achieved.

Goals and objectives will be most effective if they are reasonably attainable. It is not necessary that they be easily attainable; often it is advantageous if they present a real challenge. But goals or objectives that are impossible to attain cause discouragement and reduced effort. The setting of impossible goals defeats one of the purposes: unifying effort. Goals or objectives that are unattainable immediately should be incorporated into agency plans for further development if they become more practical.

Where possible, goals and objectives should be quantifiable and measurable. This makes the standards and goals more specific, and usually requires more detailed analysis of the factors leading to their establishment. Quantification and measurability give a better understanding of exactly what is needed and what has been accomplished.

Unlike a public works agency that can set specific tangible objectives, police agencies perform many activities that have intangible results. Efforts should be made to quantify and measure goals and objectives when possible.

Development of Goals and Objectives

The police chief executive alone can establish goals and objectives. All employees within the agency, particularly employees at the execution level, can contribute to the understanding of the problems. These employees have face-to-face contact with members of the community and are coping with problems in the field. They, in turn, will understand the problems to be met only through contact and discussion of the problems with members of the community.

Obtaining input from within the agency requires an atmosphere that encourages all employees, regardless of rank, to submit ideas. Such an atmosphere must be genuine; it must start at the top and permeate the entire agency. Employees should understand that their evaluation of the problem, their analysis of cause and their suggestions of possible solutions are all needed. Some departments have formalized this process by establishing task forces composed of personnel of all ranks, with emphasis on the lower ranks, to work out solutions to problems in certain areas. This task force approach, using only two to three officers in a small department, is feasible.

Other agencies of government often are a good source of ideas and assistance, as are community and service organizations. In order to obtain a response that is representative of the community, the police agency should take care to solicit input from private as well as official sources. Additionally, and of utmost importance, the goals and objectives of the police department must be directed by the policies of the governing body that provides formal authority for the police function.

Community meetings can be valuable for providing private input, although in some cases there is a disappointingly small number of people involved in community activity. Furthermore, those responding have not always been representative of the community, and in some cases response from community meetings does not always reach the top of the police agency. The latter is always a risk if the chief does not attend the community meetings.

Internal Publication of Goals and Objectives

No goal or objective, no matter how well founded or how well articulated, will be of value to the agency unless it is published and disseminated among the agency personnel who will be responsible for achieving it. Each employee must know what the goals and objectives are; he must understand them or be able to refer to them if in doubt. Only then can he work effectively with other employees and direct his efforts toward achieving those goals and objectives.

Review and Revision of Goals and Objectives

Chiefs should use the goals and objectives to measure progress and to indicate where additional direction might be needed. A periodic review of all goals and objectives and a written progress report assures that proper attention is provided.

In conjunction with annual budget preparation and justification, the chief executive should require that all agency goals and objectives be reviewed, evaluated and revised where appropriate. This permits reevaluation of priorities in terms of available funding. If a goal or objective does not have sufficient priority to merit funding, it should be modified, postponed or abandoned.

Review Questions - Chapter 4

1. In order to achieve goals and objectives within an organization it is imperative that these goals be
   a. short term.
   b. distributed to agency personnel.
   c. long-range.
   d. developed by the police chief.

2. When formulating goals and objectives, the goals and objectives should be directly responsive to
   a. departmental needs.
   b. political considerations.
   c. budgetary constraints.
   d. community needs.

Chapter 5
Establishment of Policy

Policy embodies the philosophies, principles, attitudes, values and intentions of management. It can be expressed orally or in writing, or it can be implied as a result of longstanding practices. Policy guides objective-directed performance.

The governing body that provides formal authority for the police function establishes basic policy both explicitly and through budgetary allocations. Consistent with the policies of local government, the police chief executive should develop policy to guide employees. Where the police chief executive is silent, the next lower person in the hierarchy may develop his policy. Where there is no policy established by higher authority, the field police officer may develop his own policy, which may not be consistent with that desired by the governing body or police chief executive.

Policy is different from rules and procedures. Policy should be stated in broad terms to guide employees. It sets limits of discretion. A policy statement deals with the principles and values that guide the performance of activities directed toward the achievement of agency objectives. A procedure is a way of proceeding—a routine—to achieve an objective. Rules significantly reduce or eliminate discretion by specifically stating what must and must not be done.

The difference between policies, procedures and rules might be illustrated in an agency's decision to identify the true level of crime. That decision would require an agency policy to report crime honestly. A number of procedures might then be established describing how reports are to be completed and approved. Finally, rules might be established to set limits on the conduct of personnel following these procedures. For example, a rule might require a written report each time a radio car is dispatched to a reported crime, whether a crime is found to have been committed or not.

Form of Policy

Policy should be clear and positive so it can be understood by everyone in the organization. Policies are tools for directing employees toward uniform goals and objectives.

If a policy is not in writing, it cannot be considered a firm commitment and personnel cannot be held strictly accountable to it. Some argue that certain policies should be unwritten to protect confidential police operations. Other argue that written policy increases civil liability by identifying a standard of care that may be used against the agency in civil actions. Nevertheless, the value of written policy to police agencies far outweighs any disadvantages.

Written policy provides the employee with guidance and direction to assist him in determining his course of action and to protect him when he takes that course. Written policy promotes uniformity and aids coordination among individuals and units of the agency. Policy promotes continuity: transmitting the agency's customs, traditions and heritage to new employees, serving as a training aid for all instructors, and promoting understanding by eliminating the distortion that can result from verbal communication.

Written policy aids supervisors in making fair and consistent decisions. Employees know what is expected of them.

Written policy must include enough detail to ensure that the action it directs will produce the desired result, but not so much detail that it unnecessarily limits the exercise of discretion. Articulating exact expressions of intent or attitude is not an easy task, but this is no excuse for a police chief executive not to provide his agency with necessary direction.

Employee Participation in Policy

Command, middle management and supervisory employees—particularly those whose units will be working within the policy guidelines—should be formally involved in policy development. If formal participation at the level of execution is impractical, informal means should be used. Some agencies hold informal meetings between the police chief executive and basic rank employees. Other agencies have used idea incentive programs and anonymous questionnaires. The method is not important as long as valid input is obtained and the employees are aware their contributions are valued. Civilian employees should not be overlooked either. They are an integral part of the police agency and can make valuable contributions to its success.

The means used to obtain policy formulation input from outside the police agency are essentially the same as those used to obtain input in developing agency goals and objectives. Formal and informal contacts with government agencies, business and professional groups, labor organizations, other private groups or individuals known to have interest or expertise, police-community meetings and community surveys are among the means that might be used.

Ultimate responsibility for formulation and dissemination of policy remains with the police chief executive. If he is to be held responsible for the performance of his agency, he must have the authority to articulate and effectuate policy.

Where Policy is Needed

Goals and objectives established without formal written policy to guide the agency's activities will never be achieved. To be effective, policy must cover all areas of the police operation in which direction is needed. Although incomplete written policy is better than no written policy at all, it can be disconcerting to an employee who has to perform without complete guidelines, not knowing whether he will be entirely on his own. Policy is a guideline for effective decision-making, and the chief executive owes the employee the stability and security of the well-defined policy necessary to make decisions or exercise discretion.

Many police chief executives have intentionally avoided establishing written policy in such sensitive areas as the use of force, particularly the use of weapons, because they fear criticism of the policy and other repercussions that could follow employee actions within the scope of the policy. However, employee actions are less apt to have adverse consequences if employees are guided by sound, written policy.

Most agencies incorporate their policy statements into the agencies' written procedures and rules. Policy compiled into a single document offers the advantage of convenience if one is specifically interested only in policy on a given subject. Combining policies, procedures and rules offers the advantage of providing all directions on a given subject in one place, but with the accompanying disadvantage of mixing inflexible rules with flexible policy. However, format is not critical as long as policy is clearly set out in a form understandable to all employees.

1. In a police department, the responsibility of developing policy to guide police employees belongs to
   a. *the mayor.*
   b. *the town council.*
   c. *the patrol sergeant.*
   d. *the police chief.*

2. In order to be most effective and beneficial a policy must be
   a. *in writing.*
   b. *fair and consistent.*
   c. *well-defined and complete.*
   d. *agreed upon by the officers.*

3. An important part of the decision-making process in policy formation within a police organization that is frequently overlooked is
   a. *the supervisory employees.*
   b. *the civilian employees.*
   c. *the state and local laws.*
   d. *the elected officials.*

Chapter 6
Written Directives Systems[1]

If police officers are to be held accountable for carrying out their assigned duties properly, they must know exactly what is expected of them. They have a right to know these expectations and command personnel have a responsibility to communicate clearly departmental standards of performance. These standards should be clearly stated as written directives.

The importance of written directives as a tool for conveying management expectations and performance standards cannot be overestimated. Directives establish a specific code of acceptable behavior as well as guide the officer in decision making by narrowing the range of acceptable discretionary action. Directives also serve as an official notice of the position of the chief on specific issues. With a properly established directive system, controversy about official department policy on critical and sensitive issues is decreased. When policies are transformed into written procedures, a foundation for standardized action is created.

System Design

The following factors are among the basic requirements of an effective written directive system:

1. Only the chief typically has the authority and responsibility to promulgate directives that explain departmental goals. The chief may also issue directives intended specifically for one departmental unit or a specific group of officers.
2. Command officers and line supervisors have the responsibility and authority to develop written directives applicable to their units' objectives in line with departmental goals.

3. Command expectations of officer conduct must be clearly stated if personnel are to be held accountable for carrying out assigned tasks.
4. All personnel, regardless of assignment, have the right to know exactly what is expected of them.

Written directives are usually divided into several categories by function. Some directives are informational in nature, while others are authoritative, defining "do's" and "don't's." Written directives basically can be divided into four commonly used categories: policies, procedures, rules and supplementary materials.

Policies. Policies summarize a department's position on the direction or limitations of agency authority in specific matters. Policies guide the organization toward achieving its goal and reflect an overall plan for the department. The following is an example of policy statement regarding the reception of citizen complaints against police officers.

It shall be the policy of this department to accept, record and investigate all complaints alleging misconduct by departmental personnel or complaints against departmental procedures, policy or the manner in which police service is delivered.

Policy is based on the views of police administrators, police ethics and experience, the desires of the community and its leaders, the results of research and the mandate of the law. Policy informs the public as well as the officers of any agency about the principles to be upheld in the performance of the police function.

Procedures. Procedures are written directives that describe expected methods of operation. While policy is a guide to thinking, procedures are guides to action.

Procedures differ from policy in that they direct attention to the performance of a specific task within the guidelines of policy. Policy establishes limits of actions while procedure directs responses within those limits. As such, a procedure is a method of performing an operation or a manner of proceeding on a course of action. For example, a general order or standard operating procedure to implement the policy on reception of citizen complaints would describe what reporting form is to be used, where copies of the complaint are to be routed, who investigates the complaint, etc.

Procedures generally permit limited flexibility within boundaries established in the directive. Since procedures are organization-wide, cutting across divisional lines, they must be promulgated under the authority of the chief executive.

There are two types of procedures:

1. General Orders/Standard Operation Procedures—These are permanent procedural directives which can be modified only by the authority of the chief executive and are in effect until so altered or suspended by another order.

2. Special Operating Orders—These are intended to define specific policy and direct procedures for special situations or events. These orders cover temporary situations and therefore lose their authority once the situation ceases to exist.

Rules. A rule directs the specific actions of police officers. The essence of a rule is its inflexibility. Rules cover situations where no deviations or exceptions are permitted. Violation of a rule generally results in disciplinary action. For example, a rule regarding reception of citizen complaints is as follows:

Officers shall courteously and promptly record in writing any complaint made by a citizen against any officer of the department. Officers may attempt to resolve the complaint, but shall never attempt to dissuade any citizen from lodging a complaint against any officer of the department. Officers shall follow established departmental procedures for processing complaints.

Due to its inflexibility, a rule is only justified when there is an unchanging feature in a situation. Rules should apply equally to all personnel. For example, the "no smoking" rule in certain areas of hospitals may exist because of the flammable or explosive nature of materials present. No individual, whether he is the hospital administrator, doctor, patient or visitor may be allowed an exception to the rule.

Rules do not allow for individual discretion, initiative or judgment. Therefore, when a department has too many rules, officers are prone to feel that the command personnel are either incapable of exercising discretion or hesitant to allow other personnel to exercise discretion. Officers may then feel that they are the tools of management rather than partners in a combined operation. Rules should be reviewed periodically to determine whether any modifications are needed.

Supplementary Material. Instructional material and memoranda, while often extensions of standard operating procedures and rules should be kept separate from the policy, procedures and rules manuals. For example, training bulletins provided to department personnel are typically instructional materials designed to supplement, support or explain rules. Memoranda are designed to either inform or direct personnel. Because these directives are usually addressed to a particular officer or unit, a formal order is not warranted.

Establishing Directives

Meaningful, effective directives are difficult to create and promulgate, particularly since periodic review of all directives is required. Application of the following factors reduces the difficulty of establishing and maintaining a written directive system.

Directives Must be Legal. Since a directive must be able to withstand courtroom challenge, comprehensive legal research should precede the issuance of any directive. In agencies with legal advisors, a staff attorney may be assigned to perform this function. In other departments, the city or county attorney should be consulted. Also, any changes in the law must be incorporated into existing directives.

Directives Must be Understandable. A directive should clearly state the intentions of the chief. The language of the directive should be precise so that it cannot be misinterpreted. Imprecise language in a directive not only hinders officers in achieving agency objectives, but also leads to litigation where final interpretation of a directive may be decided by the courts. An officer who encounters directives difficult to understand should inform his supervisor of the problem. The directive should then be reviewed to determine whether revision is required.

Directives Must be Current. Directives should be reviewed periodically to ensure they remain compatible with departmental goals and objectives. Such reviews reveal outdated directives, often in contradiction with new procedures, and other problems associated with specific directives. Operational personnel should assist in keeping directives current. For example, when an officer develops a new technique or procedure, he should suggest that it be considered for department-wide use.

Directives Should Reflect Officer Participation. Officer attitude toward directives often depends on the extent of his participation in the goal-setting and decision-making process. Officer participation is important in developing an effective directive system. Giving officers a voice in the work process tends to raise self-esteem and improve general performance.

Officers have keen insight into how proposed rules and procedures will influence their work. Often only the officer can anticipate problems in the delivery of police services created by a directive. Participation at all organizational levels in the development of directives increases commitment and creates a more positive attitude toward the written directive system. Although there are times when unpopular positions must be taken to achieve departmental goals, officer acceptance and compliance are more likely if they have participated in formulating the goals.

Officers should work to create a participatory setting within the police department. Officers should be appointed to task forces that periodically review directives. Also, officers should serve on a permanent task force, representative of all agency levels, which acts as a sounding board for new directives. A suggestion system that encourages officers to submit questions and observations concerning agency directives is an effective means of encouraging participation. Effective communication among all personnel is imperative to ensure that inquiries and suggestions are responded to promptly and appropriately.

Standards and Controls

A written directive system must be properly implemented and controlled to be effective. The directives must be recognized by all personnel as being authoritative instruments of departmental policy, and they must be prepared and issued in an organized fashion. Frequent complaints made about written directives are that directives are too numerous, are not prioritized and are constantly changing.

Authority to Issue Directives Must be Controlled. Directives that affect an entire police department should be issued only by the chief executive. Although supervisors must have a uniform means of transmitting directives to individuals in their command, only directives that affect the individual organizational entities may be issued by unit commanders. There must be no conflict between agency-wide directives issued by the chief and the unit directives issued by a supervisor or commander.

A Classification and Numbering System Must be Established. Directives should be classified for easy reference to encourage use and avoid confusion. The most common classification error occurs with general orders. Such directives carry the same force and authority as agency rules and regulations, but are issued and changed more frequently. Therefore, it is important that a system of easy classification, retention and accessibility be established.

One method of classification is to group the orders into separate categories (investigation, legal, patrol, traffic), assign a consecutive master number to each category and then assign consecutive numbers to the directives as they are issued.

Two indexing methods are needed for this system. There should be a sequential numerical index to identify directives as well as an alphabetical listing of the directives.

Distribution of Directives. Every officer who is affected by a directive should receive a personal copy. Supervisors can distribute copies of the directive to their personnel. As the directive is distributed, each subordinate indicates receipt by signing a control form. An alternative method is to place new directives in each officer's departmental mailbox. Every six months a memorandum listing all directives promulgated during that period should be issued. The officer is then responsible for obtaining missing directives.

Training on Written Directives. Supervisory personnel should explain new directives to their subordinates and give practical examples of how the directives affect daily work conditions. At this time, officers should ensure that they fully understand the new or revised directives.

The supervisor should stress the significance of changes in written directives. If the supervisor conveys the impression that he is merely fulfilling a tedious obligation, the officers may feel that the directive is not important.

In most small agencies, new officers receive their training through regional or state-level law enforcement programs. Small departments, therefore, should supplement regional or state-wide programs and include instruction on the department's written directives.

Application of Directives

The basis for the administrative process is direction and control. While the establishment of policy, procedures and rules represents the act of directing, application of these directives is best viewed as a control mechanism. However, a system of rules and regulations specifying proper behavior does not itself ensure effective discipline unless there is some method of detecting violations of the rules and bringing misconduct to the attention of the proper authorities.

While most police agencies cannot afford to devote substantial resources to "policing" themselves, certain measures are cost-effective in achieving goal-directed conduct by officers. The police supervisor is the key person who ensures that written directives are followed by officers.

The supervisor should assist officers in developing work habits that conform with directives and organizational expectations. In fulfilling this responsibility, the supervisor is expected to understand completely departmental policy, procedures and rules of conduct. Furthermore, the supervisor must be able to clarify for officers specific departmental expectations related to police conduct.

The following is a model format for policy directives.

Department Policy

Effective Date	Number
January 1, 1990	(agency provides according to numbering system)

Subject
Administrative Issuance of Policies, Procedures and Rules

Reference	Special Instructions
All Policies	
All Procedures	Rescinds all previous
All Rules	

Distribution	Re-evaluation Date	No. Pages
(agency provides according to coding system)	December 31, 1990	1

1. Procedure. Departmental policies, procedures and rules are for the express purpose of providing members of the agency with administrative interpretation of policy matters of a general nature and further to provide uniform procedures and rules for handling these matters in a more specific manner.
2. Issuing Authority. Policies will, in all instances, be issued exclusively over the signature of the chief of police. Unit procedures and rules may be issued by commanding officers with the approval of the chief of police.
3. Responsibility. Commanding officers are responsible for issuing copies of all issuances to members of their commands. Each member of the division (or department, when appropriate) will be issued a three-ring binder within which he will maintain the aforementioned issuances in a neat and orderly manner.

   Each member will be required to read each issuance and to acknowledge in writing that he has read and does understand same within 24 hours of the date of issue of the policy or procedure or within 24 hours of the date of the officer's return to service should he be on leave status at the time of issuance.
4. Inspection. The commanding officer of the affected division will cause each member's notebook to be inspected on a yearly basis.
5. Distribution. Each issuance will indicate on its face its effective date, its number, the subject matter, special reference information, special instructions, its distribution schedule, its date of reevaluation and the number of pages.

Approved by:

_____

Chief of Police

I have read and understand this policy.

_____

Signature

Endnotes

[1] IACP *Training Key* #296, "Written Directive System."

Review Questions - Chapter 6

1. Written directives that describe expected methods of operation within a police organization are known as:
   a. *training aids.*
   b. *daily reports.*
   c. *inspection orders.*
   d. *procedures.*

2. In general, the individual within a police department who ensures that written directives are followed by officers is
   a. *the chief of police.*
   b. *the first-line supervisor.*
   c. *the Operations Division commander.*
   d. *the Internal Affairs officer.*

Discussion:

Written directive systems are crucial to the efficient operation of a police agency. Why should a department have a written directives system?

Chapter 7
Police Ethics[1]

When a police officer is "sworn in," he typically pledges to maintain order, protect the public and uphold the laws of the United States, chiefly the U.S. Constitution and the state in which he serves. This initial commitment of the police officer to the welfare of the people and laws of his state and country has an inestimable personal impact. As a police recruit makes the transition from private to public life, he gradually learns of the many commitments he has assumed by virtue of his position.

Commitments and Conflict

Because the police officer functions as an active link between the law and the people, he owes several professional allegiances that at times may conflict. Many of the personal conflicts that inevitably arise in policing are related to the law, the public and the profession. The following problems in these three centers of influence are merely representative of the complexity of police work. Every officer could create his own examples of how commitment and conflict intersect in police work.

Law. To understand, uphold and protect the law is a fundamental duty of all police officers. Performance of this duty is usually a routine matter that provokes little concern about ethics. A violation occurs, an investigation ensues and apprehension of the criminal follows. However, there are aspects of certain laws as well as enforcement practices that produce conflict for a police agency and each individual officer within it. These problems are local in nature but experienced by *every* jurisdiction in different form.

First, there are certain laws that, while still on the "books," have not been regularly enforced for generations. For example, adultery and homosexuality are still outlawed in some states but "violations" of these laws have been only sporadically prosecuted in recent years. These laws are ignored because their usefulness has been redefined by society. Officers usually have no choice but to ignore such laws, and this practice presents no ethical or moral problem for society or the law enforcement profession.

These examples of laws that have become obsolete and no longer are enforced point out the significance of the popular will with regard to law enforcement. If prostitution and marijuana possession are substituted for adultery and homosexuality in our example, the subject of the impact of public opinion on law enforcement becomes considerably more controversial and complex for the police officer. Indeed laws, and especially enforcement practices, pertaining to the two offenses vary among jurisdictions. For example, in some jurisdictions, simple possession of any marijuana is prosecuted actively as a serious felony, whereas in other locales, possession of limited amounts of the drug is either considered legal or not prosecutable. With no nationwide unanimity among the public regarding the legality of marijuana possession, prostitution and other "victimless" crimes, the police as a practical matter are limited by local conditions in their response to such crimes. In such cases, police discretion in enforcement policy is influenced by community consensus.

The question of police discretion, however, raises additional ethical problems. It must first of all be evident that law enforcement cannot function without the exercise of discretion. To enforce some laws perfectly, such as parking regulations, would require infinitely greater manpower than most police departments have. Some laws are so broad that to enforce them strictly would in effect be harassing citizens. Typical of such laws are those that prohibit gambling. Most police agencies concentrate their energy on organized gambling rather than on social "penny-ante" poker in the privacy of someone's home. Yet the latter is sometimes as much a violation of the letter of the law as is the former. Often an officer will not make an arrest because the offense may be of such a minor nature as to make prosecution almost ridiculous. On other occasions a warning will serve to deter repetition of trivial offenses. Sometimes a victim will not swear out a complaint, and although prosecution could be carried out in the name of the state, the costs of this procedure may be prohibitive.

There may be other reasons why a police officer, exercising his discretion, will not make an arrest. For example, officers assigned to specialized tasks, such as homicide, burglaries or narcotics, may decide not to arrest an offender in order to make use of him as an informant in pursuing their main objectives. Is this practice ethically justifiable?

There are no easy solutions to the problems connected with the exercise of discretion. Whatever solutions exist lie in the careful regulation and supervision of selective enforcement policies and in developing a high degree of ethical sensitivity in the individual members of a police force.

Public. A police department's effectiveness can largely be measured by the amount of public confidence that the agency has gained. Public confidence in a police department is earned by the collective efforts of all officers who in their actions must project an honest, impartial and professional desire to serve others. Yet almost every officer would agree about the difficulty of projecting the right "image" to the community under all circumstances. In fact, the role of the police officer with regard to the public is a source of confusion and potential ethical conflict.

As numerous studies have shown, police officers spend most of their working day engaged in community service activities unrelated to crime prevention and control. There is no question that today the hallmark of the police profession is to serve others. Yet police departments and officers often draw sharp criticism from various segments of the public, attacks that allege police brutality, corruption, inefficiency and general insensitivity to community needs.

Public support, or lack thereof, ideally should have no influence on the performance of police officers. Regardless of prevailing police-community relations, each contact with a citizen should be conducted appropriately based on specific circumstances.

Unwarranted criticism of the police, however, lowers officer morale and creates a barrier between the police and the community. Officer cynicism directed toward his job—particularly the service component—may develop and affect police contacts with citizens. Such a situation may create a cycle of mutual dissatisfaction.

Profession. The sworn officer has several levels of commitment to the law enforcement profession. Foremost, he is a member of a nationwide occupational group that in recent years has met all of the following criteria necessary to be recognized as a profession. Law enforcement is a profession that

1. Is dedicated to the service of others;
2. Requires personal commitment to service beyond the normal 8-hour day;
3. Requires of its practitioners specialized knowledge and skills;
4. Governs itself in relation to standards of admission, training and performance;
5. Has mechanisms to ensure conformance and a disciplinary system to punish deviations;
6. Forms associations to improve their collective ability to enhance service to others; and
7. Is guided by a code of ethics.

Second, the officer is a member of a police department whose unique policies, rules and regulations control his official actions. Departmental regulations also affect the officer's private life, restricting or prohibiting certain activities.

Last, members of a police agency are typically a close-knit group with strong mutual loyalties. As is true of other professions, police officers are committed to the welfare of fellow practitioners. This sense of comraderie is heightened by their reliance on one another in dangerous situations.

These three professional commitments can be held harmoniously by officers most of the time. Usually, the goals of the profession, department and fellow officers run a parallel course in everyday police activities. However, when any one of these commitments conflicts with another, the officer faces a most difficult personal dilemma. Which loyalty does he honor? Which loyalty does he compromise? For example, the corrupt or unethical practice of a police officer invariably becomes known to other officers who then must decide whether or not to report him. The welfare of the community, the department and the profession all demand that the corrupt officer should be reported, yet this remains a most difficult duty for the officer interested in maintaining personal and professional integrity.

Officer Resolution

The ethical conflicts officers experience in police work may occur at the same time action is demanded. The officer cannot pause in the course of duty to engage in philosophical consideration of "right and wrong"—just as he cannot spontaneously develop a new procedure for an assignment. Even when reflecting on past events, the determination of ethical conduct for police officers is an overwhelming task.

Fortunately, the officer is not required to devise his own procedures or ethical philosophy. Since 1956, law enforcement has possessed a written ethical code developed by police practitioners. Application of the precepts of this code reduces ethical conflict for individual officers and strengthens the fabric of the profession. The following Law Enforcement Officer's Code of Ethics, along with the related Canons of Police Ethics, sets forth the basic concepts of professional police services.

Canons of Police Ethics

Article 1. Primary Responsibility of Job. The primary responsibility of the police service, and of the individual officer, is the protection of the people of the United States through the upholding of their laws; chief among these is the Constitution of the United States and its amendments. The law enforcement officer always represents the whole of the community and its legally expressed will and is never the arm of any political party or clique.

Article 2. Limitations of Authority. The first duty of a law enforcement officer, as upholder of the law, is to know its bounds upon him in enforcing it. Because he represents the legal will of the community, be it local, state or federal, he must be aware of the limitations and proscriptions which the people, through law, have placed upon him. He must recognize the genius of the American system of government which gives to no man, groups of men or institution, absolute power, and he must ensure that he, as a prime defender of that system, does not pervert its character.

Article 3. Duty to be Familiar with the Law and with Responsibilities of Self and Other Public Officials. The law enforcement officer shall assiduously apply himself to the study of the principles of the laws which he is sworn to uphold. He will make certain of his responsibilities in the particulars of their enforcement, seeking aid from his superiors in matters of technicality or principle when these are not clear to him; he will make special effort to understand fully his relationship to other public officials, including other law enforcement agencies, particularly on matters of jurisdiction, both geographically and substantively.

Article 4. Utilization of Proper Means to Gain Proper Ends. The law enforcement officer shall be mindful of his responsibility to pay strict heed to the selection of means in discharging the duties of his office. Violations of law or disregard for public safety and property on the part of an officer are intrinsically wrong; they are self-defeating in that they instill in the public mind a like disposition. The employment of illegal means, no matter how worthy the end, is certain to encourage disrespect for the law and its officers. If the law is to be honored, it must first be honored by those who enforce it.

Article 5. Cooperation with Public Officials in the Discharge of Their Authorized Duties. The law enforcement officer shall cooperate fully with other public officials in the discharge of authorized duties, regardless of party affiliation or personal prejudice. He shall be meticulous, however, in assuring himself of the propriety, under the law, of such actions and shall guard against the use of his office or person, whether knowingly or unknowingly, in any improper or illegal action. In any situation open to question, he shall seek authority from his superior officer, giving him a full report of the proposed service or action.

Article 6. Private Conduct. The law enforcement officer shall be mindful of his special identification by the public as an upholder of the law. Laxity of conduct or manner in private life, expressing either disrespect for the law or seeking to gain special privilege, cannot but reflect upon the police officer and the police service. The community and the service require that the law enforcement officer lead the life of a decent and honorable man. Following the career of a policeman gives no man special perquisites. It does give the satisfaction and pride of following and furthering an unbroken tradition of safeguarding the American republic. The officer who reflects upon this tradition will not degrade it. Rather, he will so conduct his private life that the public will regard him as an example of stability, fidelity and morality.

Article 7. Conduct Toward the Public. The law enforcement officer, mindful of his responsibility to the whole community, shall deal with individuals of the community in a manner calculated to instill respect for its laws and its police service. The law enforcement officer shall conduct his official life in a manner such as will inspire confidence and trust. Thus, he will be neither overbearing nor subservient, as no individual citizen has an obligation to stand in awe of him nor a right to command him. The officer will give service where he can, and require compliance with the law. He will do neither from personal preference or prejudice but rather as a duly appointed officer of the law discharging his sworn obligation.

Article 8. Conduct in Arresting and Dealing with Law Violators. The law enforcement officer shall use his powers of arrest strictly in accordance with the law and with due regard to the rights of the citizen concerned. His office gives him no right to prosecute the violator nor to mete out punishment for the offense. He shall, at all times, have a clear appreciation of his responsibilities and limitations regarding detention of the violator; he shall conduct himself in such a manner as will minimize the possibility of having to use force. To this end he shall cultivate a dedication to the service of the people and the equitable upholding of their laws whether in the handling of law violators or in dealing with the law-abiding.

Article 9. Gifts and Favors. The law enforcement officer, representing government, bears the heavy responsibility of maintaining, in his own conduct, the honor and integrity of all government institutions. He shall, therefore, guard against placing himself in a position in which any person can expect special consideration or in which the public can reasonably assume that special consideration is being given. Thus, he should be firm in refusing gifts, favors or gratuities, large or small, which can, in the public mind, be interpreted as capable of influencing his judgment in the discharge of his duties.

Article 10. Presentation of Evidence. The law enforcement officer shall be concerned equally in the prosecution of the wrong-doer and the defense of the innocent. He shall ascertain what constitutes evidence and shall present such evidence impartially and without malice. In so doing, he will ignore social, political and all other distinctions among the persons involved, strengthening the tradition of the reliability and integrity of an officer's word.

The law enforcement officer shall take special pains to increase his perception and skill of observation, mindful that in many situations his is the sole impartial testimony to the facts of a case.

Article 11. Attitude Toward Profession. The law enforcement officer shall regard the discharge of his duties as a public trust and recognize his responsibility as a public servant. By diligent study and sincere attention to self-improvement he shall strive to make the best possible application of science to the solution of crime and, in the field of human relationships, strive for effective leadership and public influence in matters affecting public safety. He shall appreciate the importance and responsibility of his office, and hold police work to be an honorable profession rendering valuable service to his community and his country.

The Evolution of the Law Enforcement Code of Ethics

The establishment of a code of ethics to govern the conduct of its members is essential in a professional association. In recognition of this, the membership of the IACP first considered the language of such a code more than 30 years ago. During the 64th Annual IACP Conference in Honolulu, Hawaii, September 29-October 3, 1957, the association passed the following resolution:

Whereas, A constitutional object of the International Association of Chiefs of Police is to encourage adherence of all police officers to high professional standards of conduct; and

Whereas, A Law Enforcement Code of Ethics has been developed jointly and adopted by the Peace Officers Association of California and the Peace Officers Research Association of California; and

Whereas, The Law Enforcement Code of Ethics has since been adopted by the National Conference of Police Associations; and

Whereas, The Board of Officers of the IACP at Chicago in June 1957 did endorse the Law Enforcement Code of Ethics and recommend its adoption at the 64th Annual Conference at Honolulu, Hawaii; now, therefore, be it

Resolved, That the IACP, at its 64th Annual Conference, does hereby adopt the Law Enforcement Code of Ethics, a copy of which is appended to this Resolution; and be it

Further Resolved, That the Association does express its appreciation to those who phrased the Code in its final form, all of whom were active members of this Association; and be it

Further Resolved, That the Code of Ethics be implemented by the Canon of Ethics as authored by the IACP.

In 1989, in an attempt to increase the code's relevance to modern policing, the Executive Committee of the IACP adopted a new Law Enforcement Code of Ethics during its October 17 meeting at the 96th Annual IACP Conference in Louisville, Kentucky. Drafted by an ad hoc committee, the new code drew much of its language from the Royal Ulster Constabulary's "Professional Policing Ethics," with the permission and assistance of Sir John C. Hermon, former chief constable.

While the new code made revisions sought by many, it also raised some concerns. The new code's length was one concern—it was considered to be too long for use as an oath of office during graduation ceremonies at police academies. Additionally, there was the fact that not all of the values and statements contained in the new document were reflected in the 1957 code. Some association members were also concerned that the membership had not voted on the revision of the code of ethics.

The solution was to edit the 1957 code, making only those changes necessary for consistency with the new version, and retitle the 1989 Law Enforcement Code of Ethics the "Police Code of Conduct." These changes were presented to the membership in the form of a resolution at the 98th Annual IACP Conference in Minneapolis, Minnesota, October 5-10, 1991, where it received unanimous approval.

Law Enforcement Code of Ethics

As a law enforcement officer, my fundamental duty is to serve the community; to safeguard lives and property; to protect the innocent against deception, the weak against oppression or intimidation and the peaceful against violence or disorder; and to respect the constitutional rights of all to liberty, equality and justice.

I will keep my private life unsullied as an example to all and will behave in a manner that does not bring discredit to me or to my agency. I will maintain courageous calm in the face of danger, scorn or ridicule; develop self-restraint; and be constantly mindful of the welfare of others. Honest in thought and deed both in my personal and official life, I will be exemplary in obeying the law and the regulations of my department. Whatever I see or hear of a confidential nature or that is confided to me in my official capacity will be kept ever secret unless revelation is necessary in the performance of my duty.

I will never act officiously or permit personal feelings, prejudices, political beliefs, aspirations, animosities or friendships to influence my decisions. With no compromise for crime and with relentless prosecution of criminals, I will enforce the law courteously and appropriately without fear or favor, malice or ill will, never employing unnecessary force or violence and never accepting gratuities.

I recognize the badge of my office as a symbol of public faith, and I accept it as a public trust to be held so long as I am true to the ethics of police service. I will never engage in acts of corruption or bribery, nor will I condone such acts by other police officers. I will cooperate with all legally authorized agencies and their representatives in the pursuit of justice.

I know that I alone am responsible for my own standard of professional performance and will take every reasonable opportunity to enhance and improve my level of knowledge and competence.

I will constantly strive to achieve these objectives and ideals, dedicating myself before God to my chosen profession . . . law enforcement.

Police Code of Conduct

All law enforcement officers must be fully aware of the ethical responsibilities of their position and must strive constantly to live up to the highest possible standards of professional policing.

The International Association of Chiefs of Police believes it important that police officers have clear advice and counsel available to assist them in performing their duties consistent with these standards, and has adopted the following ethical mandates as guidelines to meet these ends.

Primary Responsibilities of a Police Officer. A police officer acts as an official representative of government who is required and trusted to work within the law. The officer's powers and duties are conferred by statute. The fundamental duties of a police officer include serving the community, safeguarding lives and property, protecting the innocent, keeping the peace and ensuring the rights of all to liberty, equality and justice.

Performance of the Duties of a Police Officer. A police officer shall perform all duties impartially, without favor or affection or ill will and without regard to status, sex, race, religion, political belief or aspiration. All citizens will be treated equally with courtesy, consideration and dignity.

Officers will never allow personal feelings, animosities or friendships to influence official conduct. Laws will be enforced appropriately and courteously and, in carrying out their responsibilities, officers will strive to obtain maximum cooperation from the public. They will conduct themselves in appearance and deportment in such a manner as to inspire confidence and respect for the position of public trust they hold.

Discretion. A police officer will use responsibly the discretion vested in his position and exercise it within the law. The principle of reasonableness will guide the officer's determinations, and the officer will consider all surrounding circumstances in determining whether any legal action shall be taken.

Consistent and wise use of discretion, based on professional policing competence, will do much to preserve good relationships and retain the confidence of the public. There can be difficulty in choosing between conflicting courses of action. It is important to remember that a timely word of advice rather than arrest—which may be correct in appropriate circumstances—can be a more effective means of achieving a desired end.

Use of Force. A police officer will never employ unnecessary force or violence and will use only such force in the discharge of duty as is reasonable in all circumstances.

The use of force should be used only with the greatest restraint and only after discussion, negotiation and persuasion have been found to be inappropriate or ineffective. While the use of force is occasionally unavoidable, every police officer will refrain from unnecessary infliction of pain or suffering and will never engage in cruel, degrading or inhuman treatment of any person.

Confidentiality. Whatever a police officer sees, hears or learns of that is of a confidential nature will be kept secret unless the performance of duty or legal provision requires otherwise.

Members of the public have a right to security and privacy, and information obtained about them must not be improperly divulged.

Integrity. A police officer will not engage in acts of corruption or bribery, nor will an officer condone such acts by other police officers.

The public demands that the integrity of police officers be above reproach. Police officers must, therefore, avoid any conduct that might compromise integrity and thus undercut the public confidence in a law enforcement agency. Officers will refuse to accept any gifts, presents, subscriptions, favors, gratuities or promises that could be interpreted as seeking to cause the officer to refrain from performing official responsibilities honestly and within the law. Police officers must not receive private or special advantage from their official status. Respect from the public cannot be bought; it can only be earned and cultivated.

Cooperation with Other Police Officers and Agencies. Police officers will cooperate with all legally authorized agencies and their representatives in the pursuit of justice.

An officer or agency may be one among many organizations that may provide law enforcement services to a jurisdiction. It is imperative that a police officer assist colleagues fully and completely with respect and consideration at all times.

Personal-Professional Capabilities. Police officers will be responsible for their own standard of professional performance and will take every reasonable opportunity to enhance and improve their level of knowledge and competence.

Through study and experience, a police officer can acquire the high level of knowledge and competence that is essential for the efficient and effective performance of duty. The acquisition of knowledge is a never-ending process of personal and professional development that should be pursued constantly.

Private Life. Police officers will behave in a manner that does not bring discredit to their agencies or themselves.

A police officer's character and conduct while off duty must always be exemplary, thus maintaining a position of respect in the community in which he or she lives and serves. The officer's personal behavior must be beyond reproach.

Endnotes

[1]IACP *Training Key* #295, "Police Ethics."

[2]The Police Yearbook, 1958, pages 325-326, International Association of Chiefs of Police.

[3]"The Evolution of the Law Enforcement Code of Ethics," *Police Chief*, January 1992.

Review Questions - Chapter 7

Discussion:

1. The question of police discretion in law enforcement sometimes raises additional ethical problems. What can you do as chief of an agency to minimize this issue?

2. In order for an occupation to be referred to as a profession, certain criteria must be met. Discuss this criteria and determine if your agency adheres to the professional commitments.

Chapter 8
Police Corruption[1]

The police profession is sometimes reluctant to discuss corruption openly. Extreme sensitivity about the subject has developed over the years because of the intense criticism law enforcement in general receives whenever specific instances of police corruption are uncovered. Yet corruption within law enforcement is no more prevalent than in other professions or within the general public. This is true despite the fact police officers are constantly exposed to situations where official power *could* be misused for personal gain.

Corruption in police departments is not limited to well-known cases in major cities. The potential for police corruption exists in all areas of the country, in both rural and urban settings. Police officers within all ranks of a department may be involved in corrupt activities. When corruption is widespread within an agency the likelihood is great that command personnel either condone or are involved in the misconduct.

What is Corruption?

Substantial disagreement exists about what actually constitutes police corruption. Some authorities consider all instances of police misconduct as acts of corruption including such disparate cases as verbal abuse of citizens and organized "shakedowns" of criminals or businessmen. "Bribery" is often erroneously used in an all-inclusive manner to describe police corruption. One veteran officer defined corruption as the "three B's"—broads, booze and bargains. The veteran's terse definition of corruption, while easily understood by all who have served as a police officer, does not adequately reflect or include the entire problem or the complexity of some forms of police corruption.

Generally, police corruption involves the misuse of official position either to commit or ignore an unauthorized act which may or may not violate the law. As payment for misusing his position, the officer expects at some point in time to receive something of value but not necessarily money. The payoff may take the form of services, status, influence, prestige or future favoritism for the officer or someone else. Because such "debts" may be called in months or years after an officer has acted improperly, "invisible" corruption may exist in an agency. For example, the officer who agrees to tolerate illegal activity by a local politician may believe this action eventually will lead to a promotion.

Developing a working definition of police corruption requires that such misconduct be categorized. Three general areas of corruption will be considered. The first includes criminal acts in which officers not only tolerate violations of statutory law but also misuse their position to carry out the crime. A second category to be considered is the violation of oath of office or misconduct in office. Finally, violations of departmental regulations in many cases involve corrupt behavior.

Criminal Acts. It is generally agreed that the depth of police corruption is the participation in crime by police officers who use their special skills, knowledge or influence to avoid detection and apprehension. Whether an offense committed by an officer also entails corruption depends on the circumstances of the crime. The officer who uses his position to carry out a crime is part of the corruption problem, e.g., an officer who uses knowledge of his beat in committing a burglary. On the other hand, an officer who murders his wife during a family dispute commits a crime that is unconnected with the problem of corruption.

As with any other profession or the community at large, a certain percentage of police officers will engage in criminal activities. Every effort should be made to prevent these crimes by eliminating the conditions that contribute to their commission; however, a distinction must be made between crimes committed by officers that do not involve misuse of police authority and crimes that are linked with corrupt police practice.

Misconduct in Office. The phrase "misconduct in office" refers to any willful malfeasance, or nonfeasance in office and may be considered within the context of police corruption when an officer acts with malice and aforethought to thwart justice.

Malfeasance is easily recognizable, consisting of any act by a police officer which without question violates the law. For example, an officer, who telephones a bookmaker to warn him of a pending raid has violated his oath of office and should face charges of "malfeasance," if not criminal conspiracy.

In contrast misfeasance by an officer is not always immediately obvious from his actions. Misfeasance is the improper performance of an official act. Misfeasance is usually observed in the performance of duty when an officer fails to use the degree of care, skill or diligence which the circumstances reasonably demand. For example, operators of illegal gambling or prostitution businesses pay corrupt officers for protection from interruption of business, and, in general, arrest. However, such arrangements may allow for the officers to arrest members of the operation when necessary, e.g., to produce arrest statistics, alleviate pressures from outside of the police department or neutralize suspicions. Following such an arrest, the corrupt officer's testimony or evidence he obtained when making the arrest may be so weak the court will dismiss the case or impose a small fine. Thus, the "accommodation arrest" is a sham arranged between the criminal and corrupt police officer.

Nonfeasance is the omission of an act that ought to be done. It is the neglect or refusal, without sufficient excuse, to perform an act that is an officer's legal duty to perform. Thus, if vice activity openly and flagrantly flourishes in a jurisdiction, the police can be accused of nonfeasance if they have not taken reasonable steps to curb the offenses.

More commonly, charges of nonfeasance are directed toward an individual officer rather than an entire agency. For example, an officer who has not taken proper steps to stop the serving of liquor "after hours" at a bar on his beat is guilty of nonfeasance.

Regulation Violations. Violations of departmental regulations are unauthorized breaches of prescribed conduct. They may or may not be intentional and do not necessarily constitute corruption.

Well-written departmental regulations inform personnel of what is expected of them. Further, regulations must be enforced uniformly in all situations and be applied equally to all persons. Therefore, regulations must reflect an element of universality that prohibits anyone from violating them. Through regulations a police officer knows how he is expected to act in fulfilling his responsibilities, how he should conduct himself and what might result from failing to carry out the requirements of the department.

Very little disagreement exists among members of departments when specific regulations of conduct governing behavior are fair and reasonable. When rules are vague or unreasonable, the department's ability to control the activities of its officers decreases. In these cases, acceptable conduct becomes what the department will tolerate and what officers can "get away with." Impropriety and corrupt activity thrive in poorly run organizations where regulations have no real force in influencing behavior.

A common departmental regulation is one that prohibits the release of arrest records to private employers. In violation of this regulation, officers in certain jurisdictions check agency files for private employers to determine if job applicants have arrest records. Another regulation of many departments prohibits officers from working at certain part-time jobs—for example, as bartenders or private investigators. An officer working in either of these jobs might be tempted to use his police position to facilitate the part-time job. For example, as a bartender he may use his official position to enforce house rules. As a private investigator, he may utilize departmental information and resources during private investigations.

Officer Corruption

Corruption within a police department is caused by a multiplicity of constantly changing factors which vary among agencies. Personal gain appears to be a basic motivation for most police corruption. However, personal gain alone does not explain why corruption is a serious problem in some departments and virtually nonexistent in others.

Three interrelated elements that must be considered in the analysis of police corruption in any department are the individual, the agency or group, and the job.

The Individual. To some observers, human behavior, particularly antisocial behavior, is understood almost exclusively in terms of "moral character" or the lack thereof. According to this view, an officer's misuse of authority reflects his personal antisocial tendencies as manifested in corrupt activity. Moreover, poor moral character is perceived as stemming from inadequate upbringing or genetic predisposition toward crime.

According to this view, the nature of police work attracts a substantial number of persons whose only interest in the profession is the opportunity for graft. This view stresses the careful selection of candidates for police work to eliminate undesirable personnel and poor risks.

The Group. Other analyses of contributory factors related to police corruption consider the working environment of the police as much as the background or character of individual officers.

A police force functions as a closely-knit fraternity of officers who depend on one another for assistance and support both on and off the job. Mutual trust and dependence are a necessity. At any time during the course of a workday an officer's safety and perhaps his very life may depend on the actions of his fellow officers. These instances may be rare but when they do occur, each officer must be confident of the loyalty of the other. There can be no second thoughts in an emergency during which an officer's well-being is threatened.

The feeling of solidarity within a police agency is typically reinforced by the social isolation of police officers. The work schedule of police officers is not congruent with that of the 9-to-5 routine of most jobs. On holidays, weekends and evenings, when most of the population is enjoying their leisure, police officers are at work. But the disparity between the working schedules of police officers and other citizens is an insignificant part of the police officer's social isolation. What makes him separate is the experience of his job and its tremendous influence over his perception, attitudes and ability to form friendships outside of the police world.

An important part of the individual officer's attitude toward corruption is the so-called "code of silence," which has been described as an unwritten rule among police that constrains an officer from informing on or testifying against other officers. It is based on the intense feelings of loyalty to the group and mutual protectiveness against outsiders. It operates through peer pressure, and violations of the code are thought to result in being ostracized from the group. The "code of silence" is not absolute. There are limits to which most officers will avoid reporting acts of corruption. Whereas petty acts of corruption, such as free meals, may be protected by the code, extreme acts of corruption or criminality will be reported.

In practice, the code of silence leads to a perversion of ethics and makes corruption possible. It shields the corrupt police officer from exposure and condemns any colleague who would expose him. Chances are peer pressure could stop or reduce corruption, and perhaps it does in many agencies. However, in certain departments, the pressure of the group protects rather than prevents corrupt activities.

Although most police officers do not engage in corrupt acts, their failure to report instances of misconduct supports the conditions that make widespread corruption possible. Honest in every other respect, the average police officer knowing about corrupt activities may either lie or equivocate about the misconduct of a fellow officer. Usually he will claim to have no knowledge about the allegation of improper conduct when confronted.

Police officers often delude themselves about the extent of corruption within their agencies. They attempt to shield themselves from observing or thinking about the problem. Remaining "ignorant" of corruption relieves them from having to make the painful decision to recognize corruption and to report it.

The Job. The general conditions of police work cannot be overlooked when analyzing the causes of corruption. Police officers in small towns often work alone, and many of their contacts with suspects occur in isolation where the discretionary power of the officer can make the difference between freedom and arrest. Depending on the circumstances, the suspect and the officer's attitude toward his job, his judgment can be influenced in either direction.

In the course of a police officer's exposure to the worst side of humanity, he discovers dishonesty and corruption are by no means restricted to those who are commonly considered as criminal. The officer encounters many individuals of good reputation engaging in practices equally dishonest and corrupt. An officer usually can cite specific instances of reputable citizens defrauding insurance agencies by false claims, hiding earnings to avoid taxes or obtaining services or merchandise without payment.

Constant exposure to public immorality and the failures of the criminal justice system frequently creates within police officers a cynical attitude toward their work and the general public. In the limitless encounters where the officer's discretion is the basis for action, this cynicism may lead an officer to manipulate the law in the name of expediency or for personal gain.

Another factor that affects an officer's attitude is the disparity between what is defined as illegal and which laws the public expects will be enforced. The entire area of so-called victimless crimes, such as prostitution and gambling, represents an intense source of frustration to police officers. In many jurisdictions, these illegal activities are condoned by the community and treated lightly by the courts. The attitude of the public can quickly become the attitude of the police in these instances, resulting in either corrupt practices or nonfeasance.

Roots of Corruption

Within the larger community of any police jurisdiction, the practice of exchanging gifts, swapping services and extending professional "courtesies" is accepted by all citizens. It is a normal part of business relations for a salesman to offer a bargain to a steady customer or for a manufacturer to obtain favorable advertising space in a magazine or newspaper by paying "extra." Employees on public payrolls also receive gifts for professional services rendered.

The payment of money, goods or services from businessmen to police officers is a widespread, traditional practice in many jurisdictions. The free meal is perhaps the most commonly received gratuity. The extra services businessmen expect in return for giving a gratuity may include such immediate acts as additional protection during business hours and after closing, police escorts to banks and frequent patrol of the business vicinity.

This additional police protection of certain businesses detracts from the delivery of efficient and effective services to the general public. An even more serious outcome of accepting gratitudes is that street-level decisions on allocations of police personnel are influenced by who is willing to pay extra for them rather than where they are most needed. "Favors" of this sort result in serious and improper displacement of police services and ultimately will represent a serious corruption hazard despite the fact that no criminal activity may be involved.

Businessmen offering gratuities may expect nothing more of the police than vague favors when needed. If accepting gratuities from businessmen is condoned, and granting of small favors is considered within a department to be of little or no overall consequence, real harm can result. Eventually, more serious forms of corruption will tend to be unrecognized or overlooked.

Endnote

[1]IACP *Training Key* #254, "Police Corruption."

1. One of the main reasons why police corruption may become widespread within an agency is
   a. *the recruitment practices of the agency.*
   b. *the code of silence among police officers.*
   c. *the apathy of the community.*
   d. *the low pay of the police officers.*

2. A major corruption problem, nonenforcement of certain laws, is called
   a. *nonfeasance*
   b. *misfeasance*
   c. *malfeasance*
   d. *negligence*

3. Which of the following statements most accurately describes the corruption problem in police work?
   a. *Corruption is widespread; however, due to the "code of silence," relatively few instances of police misconduct are ever investigated.*
   b. *Corruption is limited only to large city police departments and then primarily within vice units such as narcotics.*
   c. *Police corruption is similar to corruption in other segments of society. It is a serious problem with no easy solutions.*
   d. *Because of the nature of the job, police corruption is inevitable and should be accepted to a limited degree.*

4. Of the many elements that contribute to corruption within a police department, which of the following usually is *least* significant?
   a. *The insularity and peer pressure of police officers*
   b. *The exposure to the worst side of humanity*
   c. *The continual opportunity to become corrupt*
   d. *The lack of a departmental internal affairs unit*

Chapter 9
Police Response to Corruption[1]

There is general agreement that the disclosure of a single instance of corruption in a police agency seriously damages the reputation of the entire department and makes all of its officers suspect in the eyes of a large segment of the community. This tends to be true even when the agency has made an honest, thorough investigation of the matter and made a full, timely disclosure of the facts. The integrity displayed by a department's efforts to rid itself of corruption is usually overlooked. What is seized upon is the fact that certain officers were corrupt. What lingers, sometimes for many years after the disclosure of corruption, is the memory that the local police force cannot be fully trusted to police itself. The effect of corruption sometimes extends beyond the department involved, so that corruption-free departments are often viewed in the same light as those which have experienced corruption.

Corruption and its disclosure also have an adverse effect on police morale. When charges of corruption have been made against an agency, internal investigations and external scrutiny combine to make the already difficult task of policing an even harder job. Under these conditions, command personnel must continue to support line officers and consider each of them innocent of any charges until the contrary is proved. Management in turn needs the confidence of all officers, for an agency loses its effectiveness without rank-and-file support. However, if a department is unprepared for the type of stress related to corruption investigation, lines of support will break, morale will decrease and an unmanageable situation will likely develop.

The best way to prevent or, if that is not possible, be prepared for corruption within a police agency is to examine the subject frankly and constantly. The consequences of evading the issue are too great.

Curbing Corruption

Perhaps the most significant factor related to police corruption is departmental attitude toward the problem. To curb corruption, a police agency must first acknowledge the potential for or existence of corruption in police work and recognize that all police officers, including supervisory and command personnel, must be held responsible for controlling the problem. Second, adequate training on the subject must be provided to all officers on the temptations and dangers they will face with regard to corruption.

Management's Role. Corruption flourishes in poorly run organizations where lines of authority are vague and supervision is weak. A police department must be properly administrated if corruption is to be controlled. Perhaps the best administrative technique for controlling corruption is to stress individual accountability and to clearly fix responsibility. Failure to hold accountable all personnel—from the chief to patrol officer—contributes to cynicism in the ranks which, in turn, breeds corruption.

The failure to hold command and supervisory personnel responsible for the actions of their subordinates is always an important cause of corruption in police agencies. However, making command accountability work is not an easy task. It takes considerable effort for management to keep track of the activities their widely dispersed subordinates are involved in at any given time. Further, the special sociological and psychological factors of police work make control measures difficult to enforce. To accomplish this, command personnel must develop a system, based on the unique needs of their departments, whereby all police activity can be clearly identified by the officer on duty, supervisors and the chief.

Educating the public about police corruption and how citizens can avoid contributing to it is a responsibility of police administrators. Whenever instances of corruption involving officers and ordinary citizens occur, the public should be informed of the details of the case so they may understand the seriousness of such apparently innocent acts as giving gratuities to the police. Large segments of the public do not realize how detrimental their own actions, regardless of intent, can be to the integrity of a police department. For example, gifts given by citizens usually represent sincere appreciation for a service rendered by a police officer. Refusal of such gifts is commonly seen as more damaging to police-community relations than accepting them, and this view may well be correct. The goal of the police administrator should be to prevent the gift offer in the first place by requesting the public not to show their appreciation in this way.

An appeal of this kind seems especially appropriate when investigation reveals a pattern of corruption in which a specific class of citizens, such as restaurant owners or hotel keepers, is offering gratuities that can only be considered as bribes. If an entire category of businessmen agreed to abandon corrupt practices simultaneously, the pattern would be terminated effectively. Such an agreement requires intensive efforts by the police administration, usually in collaboration with an association serving as the representative of the occupational group involved. In some jurisdictions an effort of this kind would be viewed as naive; in others, it might work.

Supervisor's Role. An effective anti-corruption program must have the cooperation of all members of the department including first-line supervisors. Supervisors are usually closest to the problems and set the example for others to follow. The impact of an unethical supervisor upon his subordinates is usually disastrous, resulting in widespread corruption. Even a lax attitude that appears to condone corruption will encourage officers to take unsanctioned liberties.

Because supervisors frequently work alongside their subordinates and strongly identify with them, supervisors are inclined to respect the "code of silence" and are very reluctant to take action against subordinates. Thus, enlisting the full cooperation of first-line supervisors is more difficult than it might seem.

Some supervisors may see a conflict between job performance and the low morale which a strict anti-corruption program could produce if carried out improperly. However, the morale problem can usually be overcome in a short period of time, particularly where new policies are clearly stated and enforced and where the actions of supervisors are supported by the police management. Supervisors must ensure that the policies are enforced uniformly. Making exceptions is the quickest way to sabotage a police department's efforts to rid itself of corrupt practices.

Officer's Role. Police corruption exists only if it is tolerated by police officers themselves. No one has more to do with permitting corruption to thrive or making it diminish than the operational officers in the field.

Police officers must realize that all corruption, whether it is "clean" or "dirty" represents a serious problem.[2] While there may be wide support to root out "dirty" corruption, there may be a lack of desire to stop "clean" corruption. "Clean" corruption, while it does not protect criminal activity, is a serious corruption hazard. What begins as an expression of appreciation for the police officer usually takes the form eventually of "quid pro quo." The fine line between a gratuity and a bribe is illustrated well by the actions of a restaurant owner who regularly provided free meals to certain officers. One day on the front window of his restaurant appeared a large sign: "Attention Cops! No More Free Food Until You Pay This Ticket!!" Pasted to the sign was a traffic ticket issued to the owner's wife.

The individual officer can make four significant contributions to controlling corruption within his department. First, he can avoid compromising his own integrity, a matter which may be difficult to practice because of constant contact with the public under a variety of circumstances that requires the exercise of discretion. For example, accepting a cup of coffee is not necessarily improper conduct. Sharing a cup of coffee with a citizen who offers it during the course of reporting a crime in his home, for instance, could not be construed as being improper. However, regularly accepting free coffee at a place of business cannot be viewed in the same light.

Occasionally a citizen will attempt to force his generosity on an officer. The owner of a liquor store may insist adamantly that an officer accept a bottle of scotch. In this instance, the officer must try to avoid a disagreeable incident but at the same time refuse the gift. The officer should also report the incident to his supervisor, or a designated member of the department, who would then contact the merchant and reinforce the explanation why the officer cannot accept the gift. The merchant could be thanked for his consideration.

A second contribution that officers can make is to take action against citizens who attempt bribery. For years, honest police officers have rebuffed bribery attempts by merely saying "You can get into trouble for talking like that." Actually the only thing accomplished by his verbal appeal was to stop one isolated bribery attempt. The person who offers a bribe to one police officer will likely repeat his actions if faced with the same circumstances again. Only if official action is taken against such persons can the cycle of bribery attempts be broken.

It is recognized that bribery cases under these conditions are difficult to pursue. At a minimum, the officer needs to be familiar with the elements of the offense and be able to discuss the offer with the bribe-maker in a manner that avoids entrapment.

Another effort each officer can make is to remain unsullied in his private life. For example, a police officer who overextends himself financially makes himself vulnerable to corruptive attempts by others.

The fourth step individual officers can take to curb corruption is first to recognize it and then use peer pressure to discourage corrupt conduct. Officers must make sure that they do not delude themselves about the existence of corruption or the serious consequences it can have on the entire department. Honest officers must actively seek to eliminate corruptive influences. Acceptance of corruption only encourages the dishonest officers to become involved more deeply in misconduct and increases the possibility of corruption spreading to new officers. By making the corrupt officer the social outcast, maintaining a high level of morale and displaying pride in their work and profession, officers will discourage each other from the temptations of corruption.

Training. Another requirement for effectively dealing with corruption is that it be realistically covered in training programs. Most police training programs avoid discussion of corruption, often on the grounds that it is undesirable to draw attention to wrongdoing. There is the fear that open discussion might encourage rather than prevent corrupt behavior.

Many training programs that have addressed the topic of corruption have typically been inadequate. Often these courses review the code of ethics, laws relating to bribery and departmental procedures followed in dealing with corrupt conduct. Some training has consisted only of lectures delivered by departmental chaplains or warnings by supervisory officers of the consequences of corrupt acts. It is doubtful that any of these measures by themselves will produce the desired effect.

If training is to have any impact on corruption, it must explore fully and realistically all the dimensions of the problem and include specific examples of corruption known to exist or to have existed in the individual department. The more frankly training deals with corruption as a hazard of police work, the more credibility is given to the instruction and the greater the probability that the officer will understand the problem. Training should be designed not simply to make it clear corruption is prohibited. It should provide an officer with an understanding of the problem that will enable him to avoid involvement. It should seek to instill in an officer a desire to protect his integrity, not out of fear of apprehension, but because corruption is wrong. Such training should be reinforced by supervisors and discussed openly within the officer's peer group.

Corruption Hazards

In terms of their involvement in corrupt activities, police officers have characterized themselves as "birds,"[3] "grass-eaters" and "meat-eaters."[4] Many police officers may think of themselves as "birds," i.e., those who are not corrupt but who do occasionally accept a free meal or cup of coffee. Acceptance of such gratuities is not considered to be unethical by these officers and such gifts do not usually lead to corrupt practices. The free cup of coffee represents a limit to these officers, not the beginning of a downhill slide into serious misconduct.

Other police officers who accept but do not solicit payoffs represent themselves as "grass-eaters," i.e., freely accepting gratuities including small payments from contractors, tow truck operators and gamblers. These officers do not aggressively pursue corruption as a business. They are opportunists who take advantage of circumstances.

"Meat-eaters," a small percentage of a force even in departments where corruption is widespread, spend a good deal of their working time actively seeking opportunities that offer financial gain. Typically, the areas of vice—narcotics and gambling—yield the largest payments to corrupt police officers.

Euphemisms such as birds, grass-eaters and meat-eaters may serve as a means to reduce the sense of guilt which a corrupt officer might otherwise experience. For example, an officer may rationalize that he is only a "grass-eater" or a "bird" in order to minimize his part in the corruption problem.

The following few examples of corrupt activities are some of the more common situations. These few examples do not exhaust all of the possible schemes, but illustrate corruption.

Narcotics. Corruption in the enforcement of narcotics violations has increased in recent years. Once there was an unwritten rule among police officers that narcotics graft was "dirty" money not acceptable even to those who received payments from gamblers, bar owners and the like. More relaxed attitudes toward narcotics use and the enormous profits to be derived from drug traffic have combined to make narcotics-related payoffs more acceptable among corrupt officers today. Some of the corrupt patterns that exist with regard to narcotics include

1. Keeping money and narcotics confiscated at the time of an arrest or raid.
2. Selling narcotics to addicts in exchange for stolen goods.
3. Passing on confiscated drugs to police informants for sale.
4. Rewarding addict-informants by giving them narcotics.
5. Planting or flaking narcotics on an arrested person in order to have evidence of a law violation.
6. Extorting money and narcotics from dealers for not making an arrest.
7. Padding or adding to the quantity of narcotics found on an arrested person in order to upgrade an arrest.

Indications that a police officer may be involved in corrupt narcotics activities include repeated observations of the officer present at locations frequented by narcotics users without any police action being taken; narcotic locations flourishing without proper police action being taken; a pattern of allegations of evidence being placed on a supposedly innocent person to justify an arrest; an unusual number of court cases being dismissed because of incomplete or faulty court affidavits, poor testimony or nonappearance; and the suspicion that the officer is himself a drug user.

Gambling. Although gathering court-worthy evidence against gambling operations is not easy, many forms of gambling require a permanent location that is heavily trafficked and conspicuous to the alert police officer. Therefore, the most obvious indication that corruption of this sort exists within an agency is the presence of gambling operations that are conducted with surprising openness.

Police protection of gamblers takes many forms, of which nonreporting of gambling operations is the least sophisticated. Protection can be provided at the same time by an officer who is ostensibly doing his job. For example, if a corrupt officer needs to make a gambling arrest to avoid suspicion or for other reasons, the protected gambling operator may agree to select someone from his organization to "take the fall" or pay a drug addict to act as a substitute. Another method is to frame a known gambler who is not making payoffs. If circumstances dictate that the proper gambler be arrested, the corrupt officer may ensure his release or acquittal by conducting an inadequate "investigation" or testifying poorly.

One way to detect the protection of gamblers by corrupt officers is to review the quality of their arrests and conviction records. Other corruption indicators include uncorrected parking conditions in the vicinity of gambling premises and observations of known gambling places and gamblers at specific locations without proper intelligence reports being submitted.

Prostitution. Contrary to popular opinion, the police shakedown of prostitutes for money or sexual favors is not a significant corruption problem in most jurisdictions. Apparently corrupt police officers consider prostitutes as high risks, the conventional wisdom being that they are unreliable and will quickly inform on corrupt officers if pressured.

Prostitutes operate in a variety of ways. Streetwalkers usually operate on the corners of major intersections in the business and depressed areas of a jurisdiction. Bar girls operate out of taverns, strip joints and the like. B-girls typically solicit drinks from customers in return for use of the bar as an "office." Call girls operate either from a private residence or from a public phone. They normally have a regular clientele and accept new clients only on a referral basis. Houses of prostitution are now primarily masquerading as massage parlors to avoid police enforcement efforts.

The bar girl operation is most susceptible to extortion by police officers. Bar owners who permit or promote B-girl activity in their establishments are extremely vulnerable because such violations, if prosecuted, could result in liquor license revocation and the loss of their businesses.

Indications that officers have a corrupt relationship with those engaged in prostitution include the following:

1. Police officers unaccountably familiar with known prostitutes;
2. Prostitutes openly soliciting people on the street;
3. Widespread use of hotels, massage parlors and bars by prostitutes;
4. Presence of officers not on police business at locations frequented by known prostitutes;
5. Recurring arrests of selected prostitutes only; and
6. Failure of officers to supply intelligence reports on prostitutes and their associates who frequently include pimps, drug pushers and addicts and racketeers.

Tow Trucks. Since the garage or service station to which damaged vehicles are towed stands a good chance of repairing the wrecks, there is fierce competition among tow truck drivers to arrive first at the scene of an accident and solicit the victims. Corrupt police officers can substantially increase the business of tow truck and repair shop operators by any one of the following means:

1. By recommending a towing service at the accident scene.
2. By overlooking high-pressure sales tactics of operators used on victims who are injured, dazed or drunk.
3. By intimidating the victim to utilize the services of a specific repair service.

Indications that tow truck corruption exists include unexplained visits by officers to tow truck establishments; an inordinate percentage of towing business being handled by one or by a very few towing companies; observations of tow truck operators violating the traffic regulations without corrective action being taken; and officers retaining business cards of towing companies or automobile repair shops.

To avoid such corruption hazards, police agencies should ensure motorists involved in traffic accidents make their own choice of towing companies. A systematized call-up procedure developed by the police department for towing companies should be utilized when a victim has no preference. A call-up system is fair to all towing companies and helps to circumvent competition dangers and corruption hazards.

Traffic Violations. The traffic violation bribe is often one of the first temptations placed before an officer and, if accepted, can be the beginning of the erosion of an officer's integrity. The offer of money from motorists is sometimes rationalized by officers as only a display of appreciation for something the officer might have done, which is to give a motorist a break and not write a ticket. So-called grass-eaters do not solicit bribes from motorists but, on the other hand, do not turn them down when offered. The meat-eaters are aggressive about stopping cars and have developed sophisticated techniques for extorting motorists.

Parking, as well as moving violations, is a source of corrupt money for police officers. Payoffs to officers for permitting illegal parking are sometimes made on a regular, weekly or monthly basis, most often by businessmen who wish to illegally park company trucks, delivery vehicles and their own and customer's automobiles. Where parking laws are admittedly unreasonable, police officers are more inclined to enter into such illegal arrangements with local merchants.

Summary

Elimination of corruption once it has become a serious problem in a police department requires measures that have not been discussed in depth here. Few agencies experience the kind of corruption that cripples its operations to the point when an overhaul of the system, including mass firings, is the only solution. Isolated instances of corruption within an agency are much more prevalent and more amenable to discussion in general terms.

Because of the nature of police work, the typical department has the potential for becoming a corrupt organization. Few become corrupt although a small minority of officers within many police department are dishonest. Just as there is no hope that the police can eliminate crime, so there is no realistic expectation police corruption can be entirely wiped out. But corruption can be held to a minimum when a department, through careful personnel selection, professional training and conscientious self-discipline, believes in itself and in its mission.

Endnotes

[1]IACP, *Training Key* #255, "Police Reaction to Corruption."

[2]Protecting organized crime figures, narcotics and drug offenders, and other serious offenders has been considered as "dirty" corruption. "Clean" corruption has been considered as accepting payment or gratuities from businessmen, traffic violators and the like.

[3]*A Study of the New York City Police Department Anti-Corruption Campaign* (School of Criminal Justice, State University of New York at Albany 1972), p. 25.

[4]The Knapp Commission Report on Police Corruption (New York: George Braziller, Inc., 1972) p. 65.

Review Questions - Chapter 9

1. The most important factor related to police corruption is
   a. *the size of the agency.*
   b. *the departmental attitude.*
   c. *the crime pattern in the jurisdiction.*
   d. *the morale in the police department.*

2. In which area have the police failed to combat corruption properly?
   a. *personnel selection*
   b. *departmental policy*
   c. *training*
   d. *investigation of abuses*

3. To most officers, the "free cup of coffee" represents
   a. *the beginning of serious corruption.*
   b. *a gratuity that should not be accepted.*
   c. *a boundary beyond which they will not go.*
   d. *a gratuity that is acceptable under certain conditions.*

Chapter 10
Police Conduct[1]

Appropriate behavior for police officers must be defined clearly in departmental policy and regulation. It is easily understood why police officers who are sworn to enforce the law must themselves uphold it in their actions, but it is not always clear why appropriate behavior may differ among agencies. For example, "moonlighting" may be prohibited in one agency yet allowed in a neighboring jurisdiction, or personal appearance standards between the two departments may vary significantly.

The attitudes of three groups—police administrators, the community and the officers themselves—greatly influence police conduct within a jurisdiction. Regardless of these influences, however, police conduct is professionally acceptable only if it reflects conformance with nationally recognized ethical standards.

Police Administrators

The personal commitment of agency administrators and supervisors to create an agency where officers act appropriately is a necessity. Police administrators are ultimately responsible for assuring officer conformance with departmental regulations. However, departmental supervisors must take the initiative in uncovering violations and instituting disciplinary procedures.

Administrators influence the conduct of officers primarily through the promulgation of regulations. Departmental regulations prescribe detailed rules to govern the conduct of officers both on and off duty. Personnel, for example, are typically required to wear a prescribed uniform, carry certain equipment, report on and off duty at specified times and follow a comprehensive set of general orders and standard operating procedures governing the police function. In addition, aspects of an officer's personal life are typically governed by departmental regulations. For example, officers can be held accountable for associating with undesirable individuals.

Written directives define the parameters of acceptable conduct and also serve as official notice of any agency's position with respect to the enforcement of law and internal operations of the department. This is particularly important regarding official department policy on sensitive issues peculiar to the jurisdiction.

Directives should clearly and comprehensively state what constitutes misconduct. Officers cannot be disciplined for action that has not been officially prohibited. A major consideration in establishing directives or rules of conduct is that they have a specific and reasonable use. Each directive must be realistic in terms of department acceptability and enforceability. Once written, directives should be distributed and explained to each officer to eliminate any potential misunderstanding.

The small town chief and his supervisors are responsible for sensing change, averting conflict and resolving controversy where possible to minimize disciplinary problems.

The Community

Public concern about police conduct focuses primarily on situations where officers and citizens interact in adversary situations. The questionable actions typically involve the exercise of some form of police authority, such as the holding of a person in custody, searching of a person or property, use of force or seizure of property. Complaints related to such incidents are usually decided in a judicial proceeding, whereas alleged violations of departmental policy and procedures are settled most frequently within an agency.

In the vast majority of incidents that allege the abuse of police powers, the actions of the officer are legally justified and clearly within the scope of this authority. Often, the real issue is the use of authorized police discretion and the public's perception of this discretionary action.

The police are required to exercise discretion in the application of their authority because of limited manpower as well as broadly stated or ambiguous statutes. The public's perception, however, may be that of police inconsistency in the application of their authority rather than the proper use of discretion.

The community itself influences an agency to be selective in the allocations of resources and priority setting. The services provided by a police department are limited by the financial and moral support from the community. For example, a low priority may be assigned to the enforcement of prostitution laws because of a lack of community concern, the disproportionate expenditure of police resources needed to enforce such laws and the unconcern expressed by the courts. Yet, today's low priority may be tomorrow's primary goal if public sentiment shifts. Thus, police discretionary action to commit resources to the enforcement of the prostitution laws as a result of a shift of public sentiment can appear to be indecisive enforcement effort.

The shortcutting of legal procedures sometimes reflects an effort on the part of the police to respond to public demands. Thus, for example, a community demand to clean up prostitution may lead to harassment of suspected prostitutes and violation of their rights because of the extreme difficulty in acquiring necessary evidence against an experienced prostitute and the ineffectiveness of court action even when the necessary evidence is available. Some police officers may think this illegal action is desirable in order to meet public expectations; reduce the nuisance that prostitutes present; assist in the control of venereal disease and AIDS; and reduce the number of more serious crimes, like robbery, that are often committed in conjunction with prostitution. While such illegal use of police authority may be viewed as symptomatic of more complex social problems in the community, it can never be condoned or justified.

The Officer

Police officers tend to form an insular group with strong internal loyalties and pressures. The pressure to conform to group "norms" of behavior is tremendous in police work. Fear of being excluded from the group can force most officers to act as the group desires. The conduct of individual officers is therefore heavily influenced by the collective attitude and behavior of the majority of officers in the agency.

The "socialization" process that officers undergo typically has both positive and negative aspects. For example, members of a department develop a surprisingly uniform sense about the exercise of discretionary power. In dealing with misdemeanors by juveniles and mediating disputes between spouses, officers in one agency may frequently use an alternative different from that in prevalent use in a nearby department. Although the approaches used by the officers in both cases may be locally appropriate and effective, the public may perceive the difference as an instance of legal inequity. Attitudes toward misconduct by police officers within a department are strongly influenced by peer pressure. Thus, the expected level of conduct, as well as the level of tolerance for misconduct, usually reflects a department-wide consensus. Each agency, therefore, has its own character and level of acceptable conduct. Group pressure in a department censors conduct and can force unethical officers to change their behavior on the job or leave the police profession. However, if unethical behavior is accepted by the group, such conduct is difficult to identify and eliminate.

Specific Areas of Misconduct

Even the most effective police department encounters disciplinary problems with some of its officers. Violations of rules of conduct may range from relatively insignificant transgressions to acts that result in criminal as well as administrative charges. The following are brief discussions of violations that occur with frequency in many agencies.

Moonlighting. Employment outside the department is prohibited or limited in most agencies. Off-duty employment restrictions are imposed when it is the agency's belief that a second job would interfere with an officer's ability to perform police duties effectively. Outside employment does conflict with police work if it renders the officer unavailable during an emergency, exhausts the officer so he cannot perform efficiently, impairs the operation of the agency or causes the public to lose confidence in the department. Outside employment that creates a poor public image or that may involve the officer in conflict situations, such as working in a bar, should not be permitted.

Unbecoming Conduct. All departments have a general rule prohibiting unbecoming conduct. While this is a "catch-all" regulation that is applied to misconduct not covered by specific rule, acts of unbecoming conduct must meet one of two criteria. The misconduct must impair the operation of the police agency or cause the public to lose confidence in the agency. As examples, the courts have held that the following instances of misconduct are in violation of the unbecoming conduct rule:

1. Tampering with personnel records.
2. Misuse of police radio to criticize a superior.
3. Vacationing with a known criminal.

Insubordination. An officer is insubordinate when he refuses to obey an order given by a superior. However, there are two important requirements that must be met for an officer to be guilty of insubordination. The order given must be both reasonable and lawful. For example, an order to enter a burning building engulfed in flames may be legal but could not be considered reasonable. Orders to make illegal searches or arrests, for example, represent unlawful commands that, if disobeyed, could not be used to support charges of insubordination.

Discourtesy. More citizen complaints involve accusations of officer discourtesy than any other single public grievance. Instances of serious discourtesy can result in the need for disciplinary measures. For this reason, officers should be aware that any of the following acts may constitute a valid charge: rudeness, abusive language, racial or ethnic slurs, sexual or social references, disrespect and lack of proper attention or concern.

Officers who are accused of discourteous behavior should be warned that such conduct cannot be tolerated because of the impact on relations within the community.

Negligence/Unsatisfactory Performance. Failure to perform an act required of an officer in his official capacity constitutes neglect or dereliction of duty. Examples of neglect of duty based on court opinion include sleeping on duty, intoxication, failure to respond to a radio call, overlooking flagrant vice conditions and negligently permitting a prisoner to escape.

Establishing officer inefficiency is extremely difficult because of civil service and union requirements related to firing employees. Usually such a charge requires extensive documentation based on a pattern of poor evaluations or rule violations. Specific acts of negligence can sometimes be used to substantiate a charge of unsatisfactory performance.

Political Activity. The courts have determined that police officer participation in partisan politics can be restricted. Among activities prohibited are the following:

1. Using official capacity to affect the outcome of an election;
2. Serving as an officer of a political party;
3. Publicly endorsing a partisan candidate for office;
4. Serving as a delegate, alternate or proxy at a political party convention;
5. Initiating or circulating a partisan nominating petition;
6. Taking an active part in the management of a campaign;
7. Soliciting votes in support of or opposition to a candidate;
8. Organizing a political party organization or club;
9. Driving voters to the polls on behalf of a party or candidate; and
10. Participating in fund-raising activities for parties or candidates.

The following types of activities have been deemed nonpartisan, and therefore permissible for employees to engage in. Officers can

1. Register and vote in any election.
2. Express their opinions as individuals, privately and publicly on political subjects and candidates.
3. Participate in the nonpartisan activities of a civic, community, social, labor or professional organization, or of a similar organization.
4. Be members of a political party or other political organization and participate in its activities to the extent consistent with law.
5. Attend a political convention, rally, fund-raising function or other political gathering.
6. Sign a political petition as an individual.
7. Make an individual financial contribution to political organizations.
8. Take an active part, as an independent candidate, or in support of an independent candidate, in a partisan election.
9. Be politically active in connection with a question that is not specifically identified with a political party, such as constitutional amendment, referendum, approval of a municipal ordinance or any other question or issue of a similar character.
10. Serve as an election judge or clerk, or in a similar position to perform nonpartisan duties as prescribed by state or local law.

11. Otherwise participate fully in public affairs, except as prohibited by law, in a manner that does not materially compromise their efficiency or integrity of their agency.

Prisoner Treatment. Mistreatment of persons in custody might in some cases fall into the category of misuse of force and could be charged as such. However, because of the extreme degree of control over prisoners, there is the possibility of mistreatment other than by use of excessive force, such as verbal harassment or denial of prisoner rights. Therefore, a separate regulation is necessary to address this issue. The department should issue detailed instructions specifying how prisoners are to be handled, taking into consideration such factors as safety, security and personal needs.

Operating Vehicles. The driving habits of patrol officers are constantly on view to the public. Inappropriate vehicle operation undercuts a department's enforcement of the motor vehicle laws and creates a poor police image. Officers should operate official vehicles in a careful and prudent manner and in accordance with departmental orders. When driving a private vehicle off duty, the officer should similarly obey all traffic regulations.

Processing Property and Evidence. Property or evidence that has been discovered, gathered or received in connection with departmental responsibilities should be processed in accordance with established departmental procedures. Officers should not convert to their own use, manufacture, conceal, falsify, destroy, remove, tamper with or withhold any property or evidence in connection with an investigation or other police action.

Maintenance of the "chain of evidence" is essential to a criminal investigation. Improper handling of evidence may imperil the prosecution of the offender. Also, police officers frequently come into possession of quantities of very valuable property, and the department must be diligent in preventing loss, destruction or alteration of such property. Systems and procedures for protection of evidence must be established so that any impropriety is discovered immediately and the persons responsible are identified.

Intervention. Each police officer in a department draws his authority from the same source—generally the state law. Therefore, each officer's power to make arrests is exactly the same as every other officer's power. However, for purposes of administrative efficiency, some officers are assigned primary responsibility for certain kinds of offenses, for example, vice or organized crime. Where such assignment of responsibility has taken place, it would disrupt department operations for officers to involve themselves in cases assigned to other units or officers.

Occasionally, two units or officers will find their areas of involvement overlapping and possibly conflicting—as where the vice unit wishes to arrest and bring charges against a person, but the narcotics unit wishes to have the person free to act as an informant. In such cases, it should be mandatory that the decision be left to a ranking officer with authority over both units or officers.

Residence. Police officers may be required to live within the jurisdiction served by their agency or within a specified number of miles or minutes of a duty station. One problem that frequently arises with a residence requirement is the officer who establishes a "residence of convenience" within the jurisdiction, such as a post office box or infrequently used apartment, but continues to live outside of the jurisdiction. Supervisors faced with this situation should determine the officer's true domicile—his or her permanent home.

Labor Activities. An officer cannot be disciplined or discriminated against for joining a labor union. A labor union is defined as an organization that has as its primary purpose the improvement of employee wages, hours and terms and conditions of employment. An "employee association" is not substantively different from a union unless it is a purely social group and does not seek to represent members' interests with an employer.

One form of labor activity unquestionably prohibited is the strike. The term "strike" as used here includes any form of concerted employee work stoppage designed to have an impact on the employer's setting of wages, hours or terms and conditions of employment. Striking is universally prohibited by both statutory and common law and departmental rules. Departmental policy should explicitly forbid police personnel from striking and establish appropriate measures for disciplining any violations of the no-strike policy.

Personal Associations. A police officer's right to associate with persons or groups of his choice can be limited only when the association impairs the operation of the agency or causes the public to lose confidence in the agency. An impairment will result where the association in question results in a loss of efficiency. For example, courts have held that an officer's association with a person who had a criminal record and who was the object of a narcotics investigation constitutes grounds for disciplinary action.

Supervisors should realize that persons who have had notoriously bad characters or reputations may have been rehabilitated. Also, some personal relationships are unavoidable, such as when a member of the officer's family is included within the prohibited associations. A supervisor who becomes aware of a subordinate's undesirable association should consult with the command staff before taking any action.

Changing Procedures

Since the promulgation of certain rules or procedures can generate considerable conflict between employees and management, it is desirable that input regarding rules of conduct and disciplinary procedures be solicited from all levels of an agency.

One method is the appointment of a task force consisting of personnel from every rank to examine current regulations and determine if changes are needed. Such a task force would be most effective as a permanent body so that problems and new developments could be acted on swiftly.

The input of patrol officers and first-line supervisors is of great importance since they typically understand best the practical consequences of departmental policy. Opinions and suggestions from these personnel can be actively sought. Open and frank discussions between management and employees greatly assist the creation of mutually workable directives concerning police conduct.

Endnote

[1]IACP, *Training Key* #297, "Police Conduct."

1. Every police officer in a police department draws his authority from
   a. *the police chief.*
   b. *the state law.*
   c. *the town manager.*
   d. *the police academy.*

2. The primary base that supports ethical conduct within a police agency is
   a. *supervisory control.*
   b. *written directives.*
   c. *community support.*
   d. *local statutes.*

3. In which one of the following political activities can an officer participate?
   a. *He may serve as an officer in a political party.*
   b. *He may initiate a partisan nominating petition.*
   c. *He may sign a political petition as an individual.*
   d. *He may solicit votes for or against a political candidate.*

4. Three groups whose attitudes greatly influence police conduct within a jurisdiction are
   a. *police administrators, police officers and the community.*
   b. *police officers, judges and politicians.*
   c. *police administrators, merchants and judges.*
   d. *police officers, politicians and merchants.*

Chapter 11
Guidelines for Taking Disciplinary Action

Discipline[1] is the process by which the employer ensures that each employee's conduct conforms to standards set by the employer. In police departments, these standards are generally set forth in written rules called rules of conduct.

When an employee violates a written rule, the employer has two options to ensure that the employee's future conduct conforms to departmental standards. First, the employer can take negative action, which consists of punishment of the employee for his violation of rules. Negative discipline can include an oral or written reprimand, suspension, demotion or discharge. The other alternative is positive action, in which the supervisor attempts to deal with the employee's misconduct through encouragement and persuasion. Forms of positive discipline include counseling, training and professional assistance. The application of positive and negative discipine in specific situations will be explored in greater detail below.

A good supervisor always weighs the circumstances and decides whether to apply positive or negative discipline. The tests are whether or not employee behavior can be changed by positive discipline and whether or not the severity of the offense is such that negative discipline is necessary.

The Supervisor's Role in the Disciplinary Process

The police supervisor is the key to effective discipline in the organization. It is management's responsibility to delineate the supervisor's scope of authority in taking disciplinary action. Likewise, it is each supervisor's responsibility to be aware of that authority and its limitations. The supervisor performs four basic functions in maintaining discipline among his subordinates.

The supervisor must ensure that employees do not develop work habits that will result in violations of management expectations generally and written rules of conduct specifically. In fulfilling this responsibility, the supervisor is expected fully to understand departmental policy, procedures and rules of conduct. Furthermore, the supervisor must be able to explain unclear expectations to subordinates.

The supervisor must determine whether or not alleged violations of work rules have in fact been committed by employees. Such allegations come to the supervisor's attention in various ways. They are the result of direct observation, or they may be reported by citizens or fellow employees. Discovery of such violations places the supervisor in a sensitive position because it may become the supervisor's responsibility to investigate and either take direct disciplinary action or recommend action. This often causes the supervisor considerable discomfort (especially new supervisors) because of his comradeship with other police employees. Nonetheless, the supervisor must remember that with authority comes responsibility for seeing that work is performed in accordance with management expectations.

The degree to which a supervisor must investigate a violation will depend on the immediate circumstances of the offense and departmental policy regarding division of investigative responsibility. Departmental policy and procedures may, for example, require immediate notification to the chief of police of serious employee misconduct. However, all investigations of alleged misconduct, should proceed along established guidelines assuring that the alleged offending employee not be denied any legal rights. Also, any labor contract provisions relating to misconduct investigation must be followed. Thus, to investigate effectively, the agency must establish a standard operating process, and the supervisor must be aware of the investigatory techniques to be utilized.

Once the supervisor has determined that an employee has, in fact, committed a violation of work rules, it is his duty to assess the appropriate disciplinary action that fits the violation.

As with investigating alleged employee violations of work rules, the supervisor must be aware of the limits of his authority. It is, therefore, incumbent upon management to establish clear supervisory directives specifying the supervisor's authority to discipline. Obviously, if the supervisor's authority is limited to counseling or issuing oral and written reprimands, the supervisor does not have the power to order a suspension. Equally important, a wise supervisor does not threaten disciplinary action beyond which he is authorized to take.

In carrying out these four disciplinary functions, the supervisor must aply four significant principles:

1. *The supervisor's actions must be legal.* The supervisor can take no action that contravenes federal, state or local law or court decisions that have

interpreted those laws. For example, a supervisor could not order an employee to resign from membership in the police union or other labor organizations and take disciplinary action for the employee's failure to do so, since an employee's right to join labor organizations is protected by the First Amendment freedom of assembly and the Fourteenth Amendment Due Process Clause.

2. *The supervisor's actions must be reasonable.* The supervisor's actions in the disciplinary process must be those that any reasonable and prudent supervisor would take under similar circumstances. For example, a supervisor's recommendation that an officer receive five days off for failure to have polished shoes would undoubtedly be considered excessive and unreasonable. It would also be unreasonable for a supervisor who is investigating minor employee misconduct to order an employee to come to the police station on a vacation day. Reasonableness often amounts to use of common sense in taking action. But what is common sense to one person may not be to another. Therefore, a department must establish procedures for dealing with employee discipline. The supervisor's responsibility is to carry out these procedures.

3. *The supervisor's actions must be consistent.* Inconsistent application of discipline is one of the greatest complaints from officers. The supervisor must treat all employees in the same manner, and all supervisors within the organization must act consistently as a group. A supervisor cannot allow personal bias toward an individual officer to influence the manner in which he disposes of a rule violation. Also, all supervisors in the organization must as a group consistently enforce rules of conduct and recommend disciplinary action in a manner that is perceived as being consistent by employees.

4. *The supervisor's actions must be timely.* When a violation of conduct rules occurs, the supervisor must take timely action. Acting on an offense a week, two weeks or months after the occurrence may result in a strained superior-subordinate relationship.

The Causes and Symptoms of Employee Misconduct

In order to deal effectively with employee discipline problems, the supervisor must be attuned to work conditions that cause misconduct and the symptoms of potential employee misconduct. There are several work ca potential employee discipline problem. Among these symptoms are

- Boredom,
- Discontent,
- Idleness,
- Lack of interest in the job,
- Lack of work and assignments resulting from inadequate supervision,
- Misunderstanding of policies and their need and purpose,

- Lack of uniform enforcement of regulations,
- Resentment,
- Poor communications and
- Emotional strain.[2]

When a supervisor becomes aware of these types of employment conditions, it is incumbent upon the supervisor to take steps to correct them. A failure to remedy any of these conditions will create an unhealthy atmosphere conducive to employee misconduct.

The supervisor must also be able to identify specific symptoms of employee dissatisfaction manifested by the work conditions discussed above. These symptoms indicate a potential employee discipline problem. Among these symptoms are

- Sudden change of behavior,
- Preoccupation,
- Irritability,
- Increased accidents,
- More absences,
- Increased fatigue and
- Increased alcohol problems.[3]

When the supervisor observes these symptoms, he must determine their cause and take immediate steps to correct the problem. A failure to take prompt and positive action will likely result in an act of misconduct by the employee.

Encouraging Good Employee Work Habits

An essential ingredient of effective discipline is ensuring that the work environment of employees encourages good work habits and discourages employee misconduct. Supervisors who adhere to this management principle are practicing preventive discipline, a practice that will reduce substantially the extent of employee misconduct.

A supervisor who wishes to prevent employee wrongdoing must have a basic understanding of the needs and motivations of employees. The supervisor who practices human relations will be successful in preventing most forms of employee misconduct. Following are several principles of human relations that, if applied by the supervisor, will accomplish this goal:

- Understand and practice the principles, rules and regulations that promote good conduct.
- Know employees as individuals; be consistent and treat them fairly and impartially.
- Develop a sense of belonging in the group.

- Get information to employees promptly and accurately. Help to eliminate rumors. Tell employees what is expected of them in their jobs.
- Use authority sparingly and without displaying it.
- Delegate authority as far down the line as possible.
- Seldom make an issue out of minor infractions, nor make personal issues out of discipline.
- Display confidence in employees, rather than suspicion.
- Train employees well.
- Give attention to the mental and physical welfare of the group.
- Try to avoid errors, but show willingness to admit mistakes.
- Develop loyalty in employees.
- Know that idleness leads to dissatisfaction, so keep employees busy.[4]

Investigating Employee Misconduct

Once the supervisor has some evidence of employee misconduct, it is incumbent upon him to conduct an investigation to determine the truth or falsity of the allegation. In some police departments, the supervisor's role in employee investigations is limited by the presence of an internal investigation unit specifically assigned to deal with some or all employee conduct violations. In a small department the chief may wish to designate an officer with primary responsibility of handling internal investigations. Since the chief will have the final authority on the disciplinary action, it is not recommended that he investigates the charge. Rather, he should review the investigation and take appropriate disciplinary action based upon the facts.

When conducting an investigation, the supervisor should employ the same investigative techniques that would normally be employed in any type of investigation—talking to witnesses, interviewing the employee suspected of the violation, examining relevant documents (i.e., case reports, dispatching tapes) and comparing physical characteristic evidence.

A key aspect of an investigation is the interview between the supervisor and the employee. If not handled properly by the supervisor, the interview can cause long-standing resentment on the part of the employee. It is therefore advisable that the supervisor adhere to the following guidelines when interviewing an employee regarding alleged misconduct.

The employee should be interviewed at a reasonable hour, preferably while still on duty so that he does not have to return to the police station after duty hours. The interview should also take place during a time when the employee is not ordinarily sleeping. Only where there is a critical situation dictating an immediate need for information should an employee be interviewed during off-duty hours. For example, if an allegation has been made by a citizen that an officer has severely beaten him, the immediate need for all the facts would dictate calling in the employee while off duty.

The interview should normally take place at the police station. Conducting an interview at the police station places both the supervisor and employee at ease since they are in a common setting. There will be occasions where a police station interview might not be appropriate, such as, for example, if the supervisor wants to discuss a crime scene where the officer is suspected of committing a violation of the rules of conduct. As a general rule, interviews should not take place at the employee's residence, because of the possibility of embarrassing the employee in front of his family.

Before conducting the interview, the supervisor should inform the employee of the nature of the allegation against him. It is unfair to question an employee without informing him of the circumstances surrounding the alleged incident.

Interviews should be for reasonable periods of time. When, due to the exigencies of the situation, the interview is going to extend for a long time, the employee should be given periodic respites, including time for personal necessities, meals and telephone calls.

When interviewing the officer, the supervisor should at all times remain polite and calm. No abusive or threatening language should be used.

When the incident in question is serious, such as a potential criminal charge arising out of the employee's misconduct, the supervisor should consider allowing the employee to have an attorney present if requested by the employee. In the absence of a statute or contract provision providing otherwise, police officers do not have the right to an attorney when the purpose of the interview is solely to determine the employee's fitness for continued employment (even if the alleged violation is criminal in nature). However, allowing the employee to have counsel present will not detract from the investigation so long as the employee's counsel understands that his role is to observe and not to interfere with the interview. If counsel persists in interfering with questions by the supervisor, he should be told to leave the room.

If the interview is a preliminary, informal discussion between the supervisor and the employee, there is probably no need for the interview to be recorded. However, whenever the supervisor contemplates using the statements of the employee for the purpose of proving the truth or falsity of the allegation, it would be desirable for the interview to be recorded, whether by mechanical device or stenographer. A recording of the interview ensures that there is no question as to what was said by the employee and supervisor.

Whenever the employee is being questioned regarding conduct that is, or could be, criminal in nature, he should be advised of his criminal (i.e., *Miranda*) rights prior to the interview. The rights should only be given when the employee is "in-custody" within the meaning of the *Miranda* decision, and only when the supervisor contemplates that a criminal prosecution will follow the administrative investigation. Any effort to obtain statements of the employee for future criminal prosecution should be preceded by the supervisor's obtaining a waiver of *Miranda* rights by the employee in the same manner that is used in any other criminal investigation.

The supervisor will sometimes be faced with a recalcitrant employee who willfully refuses to cooperate in determining the truth or falsity of the alleged misconduct. In this instance, the supervisor should be aware of the powers available to elicit information from the employee. *In the absence of a statute or a provision in a collective bargaining agreement,* the supervisor is empowered to apply the following investigative techniques to pressure a reluctant employee to talk:

1. *Order the employee to answer questions asked by the supervisor.* Police officers do not have the right to refuse to answer questions that are specifically, directly and narrowly related to official duties. Questions will be regarded as being "specifically, directly and narrowly related to official duties" whenever they focus on one or more employees who are suspected of violating one or more rules of conduct. If the employee refuses to answer questions, he should be ordered to do so and advised that his failure to answer can result in disciplinary action against him, including discharge. A continued failure by the employee to answer questions should compel the supervisor to charge the employee with insubordination.

If the evidence gathered prior to the interview indicates a criminal violation by the employee, the employee should be advised of his constitutional rights, including the right to counsel, if criminal prosecution is contemplated. If these rights are not given, any incriminating statements made by the employee will not be admissible in the criminal proceeding (but will be admissible in any administrative proceeding arising out of the alleged misconduct). If there is any question in the supervisor's mind as to whether there will be a need for advising the officer of *Miranda* rights prior to questioning, the supervisor should consult with his superiors and/or the prosecutor.

If criminal prosecution is not contemplated, the officer under investigation should be given the following warning if he refuses to talk about the alleged misconduct:

I wish to advise you that you are being questioned as part of an official investigation of the police department. You will be asked questions specifically directed and narrowly related to the performance of your official duties or fitness for office. You are entitled to all the rights and privileges guaranteed by the laws and the constitution of this state and the Constitution of the United States, including the right not to be compelled to incriminate yourself. I further wish to advise you that if you refuse to testify or to answer questions relating to the performance of your official duties or fitness for duty, you will be subject to departmental charges which could result in your dismissal from the police department. If you do answer, neither your statements nor any information or evidence gained by reason of such statements can be used against you in any subsequent criminal proceeding. However, these statements may be used against you in relation to subsequent departmental charges.

2. *Order the officer to take a polygraph.* The polygraph can be a valuable instrument to determine whether or not the employee's statements indicate truthtelling or deception. The polygraph should be used judiciously by supervisors. The best situation in which to employ the polygraph is when uncorroborated evidence exists indicating misconduct on the part of the employee and the employee denies the allegation of misconduct. *In the absence of a statute or contract provision providing otherwise,* the officer can be ordered to take a polygraph test and disciplined for refusal to do so. An officer who refuses to take a polygraph examination should be charged with insubordination or, if there is a specific rule for such refusal, the specific rule should be utilized.

3. *Order the officer to submit to a physical characteristic evidence test.* There will be occasions where the supervisor will need to make comparisons between an employee's physical characteristics and similar evidence found in connection with the alleged misconduct violation. This type of evidence might include fingerprints, blood, hair, urine or even the employee's body for identification purposes. Typical rule violations that would give rise to the use of this type of evidence include use of alcohol or brutality cases involving a victim and witnesses. *In the absence of law or contract provision providing otherwise,* the employee suspected of a rule violation may be ordered by the supervisor to submit to a physical characteristic evidence test. His refusal to do so can result in disciplinary action against him for insubordination. If there is a specific rule for such refusal, the specific rule should be utilized.

Another investigative technique that the supervisor might have to use is a search for physical evidence relevant to a misconduct violation. A search of this type would be of the employee's house, car or locker. A home or private car search in contravention of established constitutional principles that apply to criminal cases should be avoided. The supervisor can, however, order the employee to open his departmental locker for a search.

One sensitive investigative technique is the use of electronic surveillance (i.e., wiretapping or eavesdropping) for the purpose of gathering evidence in an employee investigation. Since this evidence-gathering technique must be applied in a manner that satisfies constitutional and statutory principles, it should be used with great discretion and only after consulting with both the chief of police and the prosecutor.

Taking Disciplinary Action

Once the supervisor's investigation indicates that the employee has, in fact, engaged in misconduct, a determination must be made as to what form of disciplinary action is most appropriate for the violation. In determining whether to engage in positive or negative disciplinary measures, the supervisor must first assess the total factual situation and decide what is most reasonable under the circumstances. Each employee's situation is different, and all relevant factors must be examined by the supervisor before deciding what action is appropriate. Factors the supervisor should take into consideration include

- The employee's past work and disciplinary history, including the nature and recency of other offenses;
- The nature and extent of the employee's contributions to the agency (awards, commendations, special projects);
- The opportunity for constructive rehabilitation;
- The nature of the position to which the employee is assigned (the more responsible the position, the more rigorous the standard of performance or conduct);
- The type and consequences of the offense;
- The possibility of misunderstanding, misinterpretation, enticement or provocation;
- The existence of contributory inefficiency or misconduct on the part of others;
- The degree to which the employee could control timing, location or events; and
- The types and severity of corrective action available.[5]

If the supervisor determines that positive discipline is, under the circumstances, the best means of dealing with the employee's misconduct, he has several options available.

Counseling. This technique involves a calm, rational discussion of the employee's problem. The purpose of the counseling is twofold:

- To give the supervisor an opportunity to explain why he is dissatisfied with the employee's conduct; and
- To permit the employee to give his version of the facts and offer information in mitigation of the conduct.

During the counseling session, both the supervisor and employee should mutually discuss the manner in which an improvement in the employee's performance can be achieved.

Training. Sometimes the employee's misconduct will be the type that can be easily corrected through training. For example, an employee's improper use of firearms may be corrected by sending him to the training academy for further firearms instruction. Other types of misconduct for which training may be appropriate include improper driving, inadequate care of equipment or poor attitude toward citizens.

Professional Assistance. Some employees with physical or psychological problems will benefit most from professional help. This type of help could include a session with a physician, psychiatrist, psychologist, clergyman or counseling organization. Employee problems that would be especially adaptable to this form of positive discipline include neurosis, psychosis, alcoholism, excessive weight or family problems.

If, after examining the facts, the supervisor determines that corrective action alone is not warranted, the supervisor has the option of punitive action. There are several types of negative action that may be available to the supervisor: oral or written reprimands, suspension, demotion or discharge.

As a general rule, the type of disciplinary action selected should run in an increasingly severe progression, with the mildest action being taken first, followed by the next action, and so on. However, the rule of progressive discipline cannot always be followed because of unique facts in any given case. For example, if the employee's first disciplinary offense is brutality against a citizen, an oral or written reprimand or short suspension would not seem appropriate.

When making a decision as to which type of disciplinary sanction best fits the employee's situation, the supervisor must take into consideration several factors:

1. *The basic penalty which would ordinarily be applied in the absence of any other factors.* The supervisor should examine the character, seriousness and consequences of the offense, the rehabilitative potential of the employee, the degree of willfullness involved in the employee's act and the degree of responsibility in the employee's job.

2. *Factors that would mitigate the penalty and result in a less severe punishment than ordinarily contemplated.* The supervisor should examine the incident of actual misconduct, looking for a misunderstanding on the employee's part, provocation by or guilt of others or other mitigating circumstances. Factors concerned with the employee's job performance should also be considered, including his length of service, quality of work, personal reputation, record of cooperation and job achievements.

3. *Facts that would operate to increase the basic penalty.* There might be some surrounding circumstances that would tend to favor a greater penalty than would ordinarily be assessed, including the character, recency and penalties of past offenses, and the number of other offenses committed during the act of misconduct.[5]

Conclusion

Every supervisor has a responsibility for knowing and utilizing the procedures established by the department to deal with employee behavior that is contrary to expectations. Most police organizations have established procedures to deal with employee misconduct. If the supervisor fails to follow these procedures, he is not conforming to expected behavior patterns and should be subjected to some type of corrective action.

The primary responsibility for enforcing departmental policies rests with supervisors. Sergeants and lieutenants are in closest contact with the rank and file and have immediate supervisory authority over them. These supervisors must clearly understand their responsibility for enforcing adherence to departmental policies, and for taking action in the face of violations.

Endnotes

[1]Lester R. Bittel, *What Every Supervisor Should Know*, 3rd ed. (McGraw-Hill: New York, 1974).

[2]Bittel.

[3]Bittel, pp. 3-4.

[4]Air Force "Discipline and Adverse Action for Civilian Personnel," AF Regulation 40-750, p. 6.

[5]Air Force, pp. 9-10.

1. The primary responsibility for enforcing departmental policies within a police department rests with
   a. *The patrol commander.*
   b. *The police chief.*
   c. *The first-line supervisor.*
   d. *The internal affairs supervisor.*

2. Which of the following characteristics does not describe a supervisor's responsibilities in carrying out the disciplinary function?
   a. *The supervisor's actions must be legal.*
   b. *The supervisor must inform command personnel.*
   c. *The supervisor must act timely.*
   d. *The supervisor's actions should be consistent.*

3. In most jurisdictions, an officer under investigation for misconduct is
   a. *Required to submit to a polygraph even for departmental purposes.*
   b. *Free to refuse taking a polygraph exam.*
   c. *Required to take a polygraph exam if criminal charges are involved.*
   d. *Permitted to waive his rights of self-incrimination.*

Chapter 12
Officer Selection in Small Departments[1]

The selection of officers may be one of the most critical factors in determining the overall effectiveness of a police department. It is the officer on the street who interacts with the public and becomes the police department in the eyes of the citizens. If the officer makes a positive public impression, the department can expect public support. However, if the impression is not positive, the result can be criticism and reduced community backing. Similarly, the bottom line for all other aspects of departmental operations depends on the quality of the individuals wearing the uniform. Therefore, officer selection becomes a key factor in determining overall departmental effectiveness, especially in smaller police departments.

Many small departments have not fully capitalized on the recent development of more effective officer selection procedures. This may be the result of thinking a more comprehensive selection process is not necessary for a small department. However, the demands on officers in small departments are in some ways even greater than those on the men and women in larger organizations. Officers in small departments must perform a very wide range of duties with few opportunities for specialization. All officers must be able to work together since a small department's organization does not provide the means to limit contact between individual officers. Individual officers and police departments are often highly scrutinized by citizens of smaller communities. Since community acceptance and support are extremely important for small departments to be successful, a comprehensive selection process may be even more critical than for larger organizations which provide more opportunity for specialization, separation of work groups and individual anonymity.

The Selection Process

Although the process of officer selection is critical to the effectiveness of the department, there is no ideal procedure to use in that decision-making process. Professional practice, not to mention federal law, requires objective selection criteria with proven validity. Yet police agencies do not have the knowledge or tools to measure completely the complex role of a police officer. Therefore, officer selection often entails a process to seek individuals with specific, desirable personal and professional qualities that would make a positive contribution to the department.

However, a number of proactive elements can be built into the selection process that directly relate to different aspects of the officer's role. These include measures of general ability, knowledge about police science, psychological screening to determine stability and ability to handle stress, background checks, and interviews by department command staff, officers and citizen advisory groups.

General Ability. A measure of general ability can be very helpful in evaluating the suitability of police officer candidates. A number of well-validated instruments to measure ability are available with a variety of norm groups so that an individual candidate's results can be compared to others with the level of training and education needed by the department. An absolute cutoff score is not practical except in the very low range because general ability must be considered in perspective with the rest of the information about the candidate. However, the police profession is demanding, and decisions must be made quickly. Many of these decisions may have far-reaching effects in the department, both for the individual officer and for the community. A reasonable level of intelligence is required to make decisions quickly while taking into account all of the elements of a unique situation.

It is important to note that an individual can be too intelligent to perform some tasks well over a long period of time. A relatively bright person may not be able to tolerate routine tasks indefinitely, and unless individuals are provided intellectual stimulation appropriate to their level of ability, the results can be boredom, depression, hostility, and of course, resignation. Therefore, ability level becomes not only data for selection but information necessary for effective personnel management once an officer is hired.

Professional Knowledge. Tests of specific information areas can also be useful. A test to determine knowledge about police science may be a very appropriate screening device for applicants above entry-level positions. A measure of interest in and potential for learning police science may be better for applicants at entry-level positions in departments that expect to provide extensive training for new employees. This is especially true for many small departments as they come to accept their role as a training ground for beginning professionals.

Psychological Screening. Psychological stability and the ability to handle stress are critical factors not only for effectiveness but for survival in law enforcement. There is no ideal psychological profile of a police officer because of the multifaceted nature of the job and the many combinations of ability, knowledge and personality that can be effective for personal and professional success. However, psychological screening can provide useful information about a candidate's psychological strengths and areas of potential vulnerability. Additionally, stress tolerance and coping skills are often indicated in psychological test results and interviews. This can be useful information for both the candidate and the management team of the police department where he will be employed. Since stress and interpersonal difficulties are often the reasons officers resign or are terminated, preemployment psychological screening becomes an important tool for increasing the effectiveness of the selection process. Also, psychological screenings are often a deterrent for many inappropriate police officer applicants, thus saving the cost of evaluating these candidates and reducing the risk of hiring a person with emotional problems.

Background Investigation. A background check is an expensive, yet necessary, aspect of officer selection. The reasons an individual seeks a position in law enforcement are sometimes not evident from the information obtained in other parts of the selection process. One's lifestyle, attitudes, self-perceptions and reputation provide important information about an individual's potential as a member of the police department. Greater objectivity and consistency can be achieved if a standard format is developed by the department for the background check and report. However, the format should not be so rigid that it prevents the officer conducting the check from following his own professional inclinations. A background check is not unlike any other investigation where the most valuable information may be obtained by chance or as a result of an officer's professional intuition.

Interviews. Interviews are an important part of the officer selection process. A resource for officer candidate evaluation that is often ignored or underused is the officer currently on the force. These are persons with whom a new officer must work, with whom a feeling of trust must be developed, and whose lives may depend on the hiring decision. A feeling of acceptance of a new officer can be initiated if he has "passed" an interview by the officers with whom he will be working. In addition, the officers develop a greater feeling of participation in the selection process and their own destinies if they are given an actual role in the selection of new personnel.

Interviews by a citizen advisory group may be an effective political and public relations technique but may not produce consistent professional recommendations. Unless the individuals involved have had a great deal of exposure to law enforcement and the police officer's work routine, they may not be able to interpret even specifically written job descriptions and departmental philosophy statements as they relate to an individual candidate. Therefore, citizen advisory groups must be trained in their legal obligations, interviewing techniques and the professional needs of the department before they can be expected to fulfill a significant role in the selection process.

Although interviews can provide valuable information and build department and community morale, it must be remembered that interviews by untrained individuals are noted for producing inconsistent employment decisions. In addition, the threat of legal action as the result of poor interviewing techniques is very real under federal law. For the interview to be an effective part of the selection process, the interviewers must be knowledgeable of the task at hand. The interviewers must be aware of their legal obligations and must be provided with objective methods of evaluating candidates.

Job Description

A job description can provide an excellent foundation from which questions and/or rating scales can be developed for evaluating applicants. Also a statement about the mission and philosophy of the police department and command staff is as important, if not more important, than job descriptions for individual police officers. The officer must function as part of a department within the community. Many of the qualities that determine the effectiveness of an individual officer are reflections of the community and the department. However, policy statements and job descriptions are often written in such general terms that they do not provide specific reference points for the objective evaluation of applicants. Statements like "serve the public interest" do not provide measurable objective criteria or even much of a basis for the subjective evaluation of an officer candidate. What is necessary is the identification of specific skills, abilities and personal attributes that enable a person to fulfill the job requirements and function effectively within the parameters of departmental policy.

Conclusion

The process of personnel selection is far from being perfected. Few decisions have the far-reaching implications for a chief as those leading to the selection of the men and women who will represent the department, the community and the profession. Since absolute selection criteria do not exist, the only alternatives are to collect as much relevant information as possible, develop objective procedures, and in the end, realize the decision must be made with less than perfect knowledge. However, the whole process builds upon itself. Through training, experience and literature, a chief can begin to determine what information is relevant, how the relevant information can be obtained, which elements can be dealt with objectively and which elements must be evaluated by professional judgment. Some of the components of the selection process described may be new and seem too costly to chiefs of small departments. However, certain things, such as psychological screenings and ability testing, can be contracted with private psychologists and community mental health centers. The cost of this type of consulting can be a good investment when it reduces interpersonal conflict within the department, limits the rate of officer turnover and improves community support. No chief can expect to develop a perfect selection record, if for no other reasons than the limitations in our knowledge and the fact that individuals change. Yet, in building a strong department and profession, the selection process becomes the foundation for the rest of the structure.

Endnote

[1]George C. Schonengerdt and Debra A. G. Robinson, "Officer Selection: An Important Process for Small Departments," *FBI Bulletin,* December 1983.

Review Questions - Chapter 12

1. What is the most crucial factor in determining the overall effectiveness of a police department?
   a. *Employment of up-to-date technology.*
   b. *The chief's relationship with political leaders.*
   c. *The proper selection of police officers.*
   d. *The department's relationship with the news media.*

2. The purpose of the officer selection process is to
   a. *screen out undesirable candidates with personality flaws.*
   b. *provide the opportunity for the city manager to approve the candidate.*
   c. *verify the information contained on the candidates application.*
   d. *find the candidate with specific, desirable personal and professional qualities that would make a positive contribution to the department.*

Chapter 13
Assessment of Applicants[1]

Most police administrators recognize the need for proper assessment of police applicants. Rapid social change and growth have expanded the role of the police officer and increased the complexity of police work. Police administrators should recognize the importance of several factors in police officer selection. These include the necessity for officers to possess a variety of skills and strengths; the focus of public attention on the quality of police performance; and legal guidelines on the selection and promotion of police officers. While some larger police departments have established comprehensive assessment center-type selection procedures for their officers, most departments still rely on antiquated and sometimes questionable selection methods.

The vast majority of police departments use traditional selection techniques, including written intelligence tests, background investigations, psychological evaluations and clinical interviews (with or without polygraph assistance). Due to the fact that a great many police agencies come under the auspices of the civil service commission, there is some reluctance on the part of authorities to deviate from the more traditional methods of selection. Despite the desire of police departments to implement more comprehensive selection systems, the lack of autonomy to initiate such systems leaves the department with an outdated evaluation selection system. With federal and court-ordered requirements on personnel selection and fair hiring practices, police administrators may also be reluctant to deviate from traditional approaches for fear of civil litigation.

Job Relatedness and Validity

One of the major problems with traditional forms of police officer selection methods is job-relatedness.[2] While psychological testing, background investigations, oral interviews and polygraph testing may be justified on the basis of job-relatedness, paper and pencil tests of knowledge may not be justified. The job-relatedness of a selection or promotion system is important for two reasons: "(1) It is more likely to be valid (measure and predict success), and (2) it is more likely to generate some type of legal action if it doesn't relate to the job in question."[3] Many smaller departments use standardized police entrance examinations developed by other, larger police agencies. While these exams may be valid and reliable measurement instruments for the agencies for which they were developed, they may not apply in the same manner to smaller agencies.

The validity of tests used in the police selection system may be one of the most important problems faced by police departments.[4] O'Leary maintains that "any selection system will deselect or eliminate a substantial number of people."[5] Those not selected may voice their reservations concerning appropriateness and validity of the system. "The basic point underlying all these considerations is the importance of the selection system being related to the job and, therefore, being valid."[6]

No single method for screening police applicants has consistently been found to be predictive of the quality of future job performance.[7] One approach to selection that has received considerable interest, however, is the assessment center. Assessment is a method of conducting psychological and performance evaluations of individuals that involves testing and observations of individuals in a group setting with situational tests and comprehensive measurement procedures. An assessment center approach points out candidates' strengths and weaknesses and is easily shown to be job-related. Requirements in the assessment center approach include the use of multiple simulations (such as role playing) and multiple behavior assessments (stress and anger levels, for example). While assessment center approaches have received mixed reviews regarding validity and reliability research, the majority of empirical research tends to endorse the practice.[8]

The antiquated selection and promotion systems in many police departments have come under increased scrutiny by the courts. Thus, there is an increased need to identify more efficient job-related selection procedures. While assessment centers for police applicant selection may be touted as superior over traditional methods, the approach is expensive and time consuming. Since most police departments in the United States are small, they may have neither the resources nor the budget to provide an assessment center selection procedure. While the use of assessment centers may deal with some of the problems plaguing police departments' selection methods, there may be alternative, equally effective instruments and/or procedures that are more appropriate to the legal and budgetary guidelines of the specific police organizational setting.

Case Study Assessment

Case study situations are a major component of the assessment center selection approach. There seem to be two basic uses of case studies in assessment centers. One approach attempts to have the applicant analyze and discuss the implications of a case situation and provide the correct or preferred answer or response (analytical). Another, less frequent type of case study presents a problem-solving scenario in which there is no clear-cut, right or wrong decision (experiential). The applicant is required to resolve the case study conflict by proposing a workable course of action. This involves the incorporation of decision making, previous experience, common sense, academic learning and initiative.

Experiential case studies have been shown to be a particularly useful tool in law enforcement education and training.[9] Police officers frequently encounter situations for which no single appropriate response or course of action is immediately known or available. Therefore, experiential case scenarios seem particularly suited for justifying job-relatedness as an evaluation instrument. Unlike other case study approaches, the experiential case situation provides a structured case example in which the applicant becomes involved, evaluates the situation, applies concepts learned in other contexts (classroom, experience, training) and develops a workable course of action or solution to the problem. The experiential case scenario may involve a multitude of situations that a police officer is likely to encounter (e.g., ethical, legal applications, crisis intervention, etc.).

The experiential case situation may be used orally (during interviews) or as a written response examination. The latter seems to be preferred because of documentation requirements and the evaluation process. In addition, the applicant's written responses may be judged with regard to writing skills, grammar, thought organization and the application of logic (or common sense). The response of the applicant may be judged by evaluators familiar with the needs of the particular police department, thereby increasing the validity and appropriateness of the evaluation.

An evaluation using experiential case situations as a method of police selection was made with five small to medium-sized law enforcement agencies (municipal police and county sheriff's departments). Each of the five agencies used traditional police applicant selection methods (such as knowledge tests, psychological tests, background investigations and oral interviews). To avoid the disruption of regular agency selection methods, the experiential case situation assessment was administered to those applicants who had been selected by traditional means. A total of 16 newly selected police officers were subjected to the experiential case situation assessment method.

The experiential assessment instrument consisted of five case scenarios and two ranked evaluation measurement instruments. The five scenarios involved situations a police officer might typically encounter,[10] and included decision-making problems in ethics, law, interpersonal relationships and logic. The officers were instructed to complete the five scenarios within two hours, using 100 words or less in each response. The completed instruments were rated by three evaluators using the police applicant evaluation form. The evaluators included one supervisor from the employing agency, one law enforcement training instructor and one veteran police officer considered to be an exemplary officer by the employing police department. The three evaluations for each officer were averaged for a total score. A Kendall's Coefficient of Concordance (W) was conducted on the interreliability of the evaluators' ratings of the police applicants. There was a high degree of agreement among the three evaluators regarding the individual applicant evaluations, thus indicating the reliability of the rating method (W=.80).

A second evaluation was conducted on each of the 16 officers at the end of six months. Since most of the police agencies in the study utilized a six-month probationary period for their officers, this was used for the present study. The six-month performance evaluation instrument was administered using the same criteria as the first evaluation rating instrument. The rating was completed by individual officers' supervisor who normally made such evaluations (e.g., shift supervisor, field training officer, sergeant, etc.). The scores of the performance rating were compared with the scores of the experiential situation assessment ratings, and there was consistent, significant agreement between the assessment ratings and the performance ratings for the 16 officers. A Kendall's Tau correlation coefficient indicated the experiential case study assessment correctly predicted the majority of the performance evaluations (Tau=.73, Tau Coefficient=5.87, p ⁶.01).

The experiential case situation evaluation model continues undergoing reliability and validity research. However, the preliminary findings suggest a significant correlation between the experiential case study assessment and "end-of-probation" police performance evaluations. These findings suggest that the experiential case study assessment method is well-suited for smaller law enforcement departments when used in conjunction with traditional selection/screening methods. The procedure is relatively easy, cost-effective and job-related. In addition, experiential evaluation results of police applicants seem to predict future performance in the field.

Police Applicant Assessment Instrument

To the Police Applicant:
   The following are five hypothetical case scenarios in which you are a police officer. [Editor's note: Only one scenario will be reprinted here.]
   Read each case carefully. Following each case are questions that you should answer using 100 words or less. Use the attached blank sheets of paper to record your answers. Do not write on the cases themselves. You will have two hours to complete this examination. Thank you.

Case 1

It is your first day back on the 7 a.m. to 3 p.m. shift. You are in the roll call room of the state police barracks waiting for your sergeant to address the shift before you go on patrol. Sipping on a cup of coffee and trying to wake up, you wonder what the weather will be like.

"Hope it doesn't rain. There will be a lot of traffic accidents to work if it rains," you think to yourself.

The sergeant, looking a little sleepy himself, enters the roll call room.

"All right men, I don't have any new items for you, but I do want to remind you about the mental patient who escaped from custody yesterday. The city and county have not had any luck locating him and they have asked us to keep an eye on the interstates. He may be trying to get home. Remember, he can be dangerous. For those of you who have been off for a couple of days, I have some copies of this guy's description and background. Pick up one before you go out. Any questions?"

The room is quiet for a few seconds. When you realize that no one else is going to say anything, you raise your hand.

"Sergeant, have you heard what the weather's going to be like today?"

"Oh yes, it's supposed to rain so be sure you all have enough accident forms," he warns.

After picking up a copy of the escaped mental patient report and checking out your patrol car, you proceed toward your patrol zone, which consists of approximately 50 miles of interstate and 100 square miles of suburban area near a metropolitan city.

Traffic accidents keep you busy during the first few hours of the shift. Your sergeant was right about the rain. It began raining just after you left the state police barracks and, needless to say, has contributed to a number of commuter accidents in your zone. It is now 11 a.m. and you decide to eat an early lunch and work on some reports at a nearby truck stop. As you start to obtain clearance on the radio, the dispatcher provides new information on the escaped mental patient.

"All units prepare to copy. Be advised that city P.D. has informed us that a homicide occurred in Fairbanks subdivision last evening. Suspect is described as being the escaped mental patient from the state hospital. Suspect last seen in the Fairbanks subdivision, running from the scene in a northerly direction at about 7 a.m. this date. Consider suspect armed with a knife and dangerous."

The report surprises you. You didn't realize that the escaped mental patient was that dangerous. You fumble through your attache case and pull out the report on the mental patient. After a closer reading, the report indicates that the individual is criminally insane and extremely dangerous. You now wish that you had read the report in more detail, since Fairbanks subdivision is only a few miles from your patrol zone. You decide to telephone headquarters from the truck stop in an effort to acquire more information on the fugitive.

94

The records clerk at headquarters advises you that the mental patient stabbed an elderly woman to death last night. The patient had broken into a residence at Fairbanks subdivision where the elderly woman lived alone with her two small dogs. The records clerk reports that the mental patient also stabbed the dogs to death.

Hanging up the phone, you decide to skip lunch in favor of some peanut butter crackers and a soft drink. You feel that you should spend the time patrolling the areas near Fairbanks subdivision, looking for the mental patient.

It is still raining hard and you hope that there will not be any more traffic accidents to work before you get off-duty. The radio dispatcher interrupts your thoughts.

"Attention all units in Zone 26 and vicinity. An armed robbery has just occurred at the Pike Street Liquor Store. Two suspects seen heading north in a 1973 red Duster. City police were in pursuit of suspect vehicle until lost near Interstate 26 and the Brookcastle Highway."

Zone 26 is your zone and you're only a few miles from the Brookcastle exit. You begin to head south on I-26, watching the northbound side of traffic for the red Duster.

You observe a man hitchhiking on the northbound side of the interstate. The man is dressed in only a shirt and pants and you think about why the man isn't under a bridge for cover from the rain. You realize that the man could fit the description of the escaped mental patient. As you look for a level area in the median strip to turn, you notice a black Volkswagen—with what appears to be two girls inside—stopping to pick up the hitchhiker. Just as you begin to pull into the median strip, a red Duster speeds by on the northbound side of the interstate. It is raining hard and you are unable to make out the occupants of the car or its license plate. Pulling into the northbound lane, you realize that you must make a decision. The hitchhiker who was just picked up by the girls may or may not be the escaped mental patient. The red Duster could be the robbers or just someone driving too fast in the rain. You have enough probable cause to stop either the Duster or the Volkswagen.

Making a radio call for assistance would result in at least a five-minute delay waiting for a back-up unit. By that time, the vehicle you decide not to stop would probably be lost. You cannot waste any more time. You have to act now.

Based on what you have read, answer the following questions:
1. What are you going to do?
2. Why?
After answering the above questions, go on to the next case.

Police Assessment Form

Name of Officer: _____

Rater: _____

Score: _____

Instructions: Complete this form based upon personal observations and knowledge. Please read each of the 10 assessment statements before filling out this form. Each statement is ranked from 0-10 using the following scale as a guide:

0	1	2	3	4	5	6	7	8	9	10
Unacceptable		Poor			Average			Good		Excellent

A total score is obtained by adding the response for each statement. The following grading scale should be used as a guide: 90-100 Excellent; 70-89 Good; 40-69 Average; 20-39 Poor; 0-19 Unacceptable.

Assessment Statements

The above-named officer   (Circle One)

1. Displays knowledge of law and legal procedures.

   0 1 2 3 4 5 6 7 8 9 10

2. Considers the impact his/her decisions might have on police/community relations.

   0 1 2 3 4 5 6 7 8 9 10

3. Understands and displays concern for ethical standards applied to police work.

   0 1 2 3 4 5 6 7 8 9 10

4. Displays complete confidence in his/her decisions.

   0 1 2 3 4 5 6 7 8 9 10

5. Makes logical and sensible decisions and takes appropriate actions.

   0 1 2 3 4 5 6 7 8 9 10

6. Has the ability to comprehend and interpret decision-making problems and the consequences of actions taken.

   0 1 2 3 4 5 6 7 8 9 10

7. Is able to appropriately justify his/her decisions and actions taken.

   0 1 2 3 4 5 6 7 8 9 10

8. Is capable of expressing in writing organized thoughts.

   0 1 2 3 4 5 6 7 8 9 10

9. Has a command of proper grammar and   0 1 2 3 4 5 6 7 8 9 10
   an adequate vocabulary.

10. Possesses those characteristics desirable   0 1 2 3 4 5 6 7 8 9 10
    in a professional law enforcement officer.

Police Applicant Evaluation Score Sheet

To the Evaluator: After reading the police applicant's responses on the five case scenarios, use this form to record your evaluation. Please read each of the 10 evaluation statements before filling out this form. Each statement is ranked from 1-10 using the following scale as a guide:

0	1	2	3	4	5	6	7	8	9	10
Unacceptable		Poor			Average			Good		Excellent

A total score is obtained by adding the response for each statement. The following grading scale should be used as a guide:

90-100 Excellent   Applicant's Name: _____
70-89   Good   _____
40-69   Average   Evaluator: _____
20-39   Poor
0-19   Unacceptable _____

Evaluation Statements

The responses indicated the applicant   (Circle One)

1. Displayed knowledge of law and legal   0 1 2 3 4 5 6 7 8 9 10
   procedures.

2. Considered the impact his/her decisions   0 1 2 3 4 5 6 7 8 9 10
   might have on police/community rela-
   tions.

3. Understands and displays concern for   0 1 2 3 4 5 6 7 8 9 10
   ethical standards applied to police work.

4. Displays complete confidence in his/her   0 1 2 3 4 5 6 7 8 9 10
   decisions.

5. Makes logical and sensible decisions and   0 1 2 3 4 5 6 7 8 9 10
   takes appropriate actions.

6. Has the ability to comprehend and   0 1 2 3 4 5 6 7 8 9 10
   interpret decision-making problems and
   the consequences of actions taken.

97

7. Is able to appropriately justify his/her   0 1 2 3 4 5 6 7 8 9 10
   decisions and actions taken.

8. Is capable of expressing in writing   0 1 2 3 4 5 6 7 8 9 10
   organized thoughts.

9. Has a command of proper grammar and   0 1 2 3 4 5 6 7 8 9 10
   an adequate vocabulary.

10. Possesses those characteristics desirable   0 1 2 3 4 5 6 7 8 9 10
    in a professional law enforcement officer.

Endnotes

[1]Ron England and Larry S. Miller, "Assessing Police Applicants Through Experiential Case Studies," *Police Chief*, April 1989.

[2]A.F. Carr, L.D. Larson, J.F. Schnelle and R.E. Kirchner, "Outcome Measure of Police Performance: Some Steps Toward Accountability," *Journal of Community Psychology*, 1980, Vol. 8, pp. 165-171.

[3]L. O'Leary, "Objectivity and Job Relatedness: Can We Have Our Cake and Eat It Too?," *Public Personnel Management*, 1976, Vol. 5, pp. 423-433.

[4]C.D. Speilberger, *Police Selection Evaluation* (Washington, D.C.: Hemisphere, 1979).

[5]O'Leary.

[6]*Ibid.*

[7]Speilberger.

[8]J.D. Ross, "Determination of the Predictive Validity of the Assessment Center Approach to Selecting Police Managers," *Journal of Criminal Justice*, 1980, Vol. 8, pp. 89-96.

[9]L.S. Miller and M.C. Braswell, "The Utility of Experiential Case Studies in Police Education: A Comparative Analysis," *Criminal Justice Review*, Fall 1986.

[10]L.S. Miller and M.C. Braswell, *Human Relations and Police Work*, 2nd edition (Prospect Heights, IL: Waveland Press, 1988).

1. A non-traditional method of police officer selection and promotion in use in many law enforcement agencies is the
   a. *employment agency.*
   b. *civil service commission.*
   c. *assessment center.*
   d. *lateral transfer policy.*

Discussion:
   How can the use of written hypothetical case scenarios during
the applicant process aid in police recruit selection?

Chapter 14
Important Factors in Psychological Screening[1]

The use of psychological screening instruments has been growing in importance for the past 30 years. As early as 1917, an attempt was being made to measure the intelligence level of police officers. Since 1950, a variety of nationwide surveys of police organizations were undertaken to determine the extent of the use of psychological instruments as part of the police selection process. Results show a growing reliance upon the use of psychological methods and techniques in making decisions about police applicants. There has also been encouragement for continued research in the use of psychological testing of police candidates.

There have been two very strong recommendations for the use of psychological methods in the hiring of police officers which have had a major impact on the level of importance being given these techniques. In 1967, the President's Commission on Law Enforcement and the Administration of Justice stated that "psychological tests . . . to determine emotional stability should be conducted in all departments."[2] Further, the National Advisory Commission on Criminal Justice Standards and Goals in a report on the police (1973) indicated

Police officers are subject to great emotional stress, and they are placed in positions of trust. For these reasons, they should be very carefully screened to preclude the employment of those who are emotionally unstable, brutal or who suffer any form of emotional illness. A growing number of police agencies have turned to psychological screening to eliminate those who are emotionally or otherwise unfit for the police service.[3]

With this statement in mind, the National Advisory Commission offered the following recommendation:

Standard 13.5.2 Every police agency, by 1975, should retain the services of a qualified psychiatrist or psychologist to conduct psychological testing of police applicants to screen out those who have mental disorders or are emotionally unfit for police work.[4]

It is clear that on a national level there has been an ever-increasing interest and importance placed on the use of psychological screening of police applicants.

In New York State, a Senate committee stressed the need for psychological screening of police officers. It stated that "the checking of backgrounds and psychological fitness are essential in weeding out undesirable candidates."[5] The committee further reports that no candidate should be allowed on a police department until such assessment is completed. They recommended a rather extensive battery and argued that "standards for psychological fitness of police officers should never be compromised. The appointment of potentially emotionally unstable individuals to the police force would be extremely hazardous."[6]

Experts stress the economic benefits of psychological screening. They note that the cost of training an officer and employing him for a year is very high compared to the relatively inexpensive screening process. Removing the unfit officer from consideration early in the process can reflect significant savings in training and other support, not to mention reducing the possible liability of retaining such an individual. In addition, an officer who must terminate employment because of misconduct or stress disability becomes a major monetary drain.

Selecting vs. Screening

The psychological screening of police applicants must be considered separately from the use of testing as a means of selecting or predicting the best candidate. Selecting candidates has as its goal the choosing of individuals who possess certain positive traits believed to be associated with effective performance in law enforcement. Screening, on the other hand, has the goal of eliminating from consideration those who demonstrate significant signs of psychopathology or emotional instability, or who lack the basic ability or mental acuity to perform the job in a safe and responsible manner.

Status of Selection Procedures

Much research on the use of psychological testing of police candidates has been directed toward the prediction of future police performance on the basis of a series of tests. Many studies have attempted to demonstrate that scores on standardized tests correlate positively with some measure of future job performance. For the most part, these studies have focused on intelligence tests, interest inventories and personality questionnaires as predictors. Criteria have included training academy grades, supervisory ratings, observations of field behaviors, accident proneness and similar measures.

In general, the results of such attempts have not been highly fruitful. Prediction of future behavior is very difficult under even the best conditions, but predicting police behavior has additional inherent problems. The major problems are as follows:

1. Since there are between 15,000-20,000 police agencies in the United States, a wide diversity in size and type of department exists. In addition, the nature, demands and needs of communities vary tremendously. Therefore, criteria in the form of definitions of effective performance also vary widely.
2. Because of the differences noted above, there is a wide variation in police tasks and responsibilities, making standardization of requirements impossible.
3. There is little consensus on the "ideal" police officer with regard to behavior and traits. Often the same positive results are obtained in many different ways, by very different kinds of individuals.
4. Finally, it is reasonable to expect changes in the nature and make-up of the police workforce over a period of time. It appears that the present workforce is more highly educated than was true earlier. It is also clear that the tasks of police officers are becoming more technical, legalistic and socially demanding. Continuous changes can be expected in this field.

Thus, it is difficult at best to develop a psychological testing process that is aimed at selecting applicants who are most likely to succeed based on possessing certain traits or characteristics. Furthermore, the psychology of human development has repeatedly demonstrated that personality is not a static condition, but that individuals change within certain limits throughout their lives. This makes specific prediction of future performance within narrow ranges of behavior very difficult and, realistically, not practical at the present time. Research needs to continue in this area and, it is hoped, will lead to more promising methods.

Screening Out Psychologically Unsuitable Candidates

In their book, *The Police Personnel Selection Process*, Territo, Swanson and Chamelin stress that law enforcement agencies are under a heavy obligation to improve their techniques for detecting the high-risk applicant before hire. A high-risk applicant is one whose psychological make-up is such that he will quite likely be unable to cope with the responsibilities and authority inherent in the position of police officer. The responsibility is placed more and more directly on the police agency to include a program of psychological testing aimed at eliminating applicants who potentially represent a risk to the public, to fellow officers or to themselves.

Psychological testing for the purpose of eliminating high-risk applicants appears to have gained rather a wide national level of acceptance by police organizations in the United States. This type of evaluation is specifically and narrowly aimed at identifying the applicant who possesses or demonstrates any behaviors or characteristics which prepresent a significant risk to the community, peers or self. As noted by others, this screening focuses on "such personal attributes as excessive fearfulness, phobias, uncontrolled inpulsivity, inability to handle hostility, self-destructive behaviors, paranoid tendencies and delusional thinking, as well as clearly psychotic conditions and character disorders. Evidence of antisocial attitudes and behaviors, and alcohol/drug abuse tendencies are also sought out."[7]

In general, clinical and standardized testing methods that are considered valid in identifying such conditions are selected and included in an assessment battery. A article points out that "the psychological examination provides an excellent balance for the oral interview and polygraph examination, and is principally of value in identifying the person who is clearly not psychologically suited to police employment. This phase of testing appears to be critical in terms of negating liability where charges of negligent admission might arise as a result of misconduct of an officer following employment."[8]

It is important to stress several points. The distinction between selecting in and screening out is essential and is frequently overlooked. The selecting in process relies heavily on the ability of the test to predict performance at a later time. Long-term predictions are highly desired, but not very reliable. The screening-out process, on the other hand, relies on the ability of an instrument or technique to assess the individual's behavior at the present time. This process is more reliable and can be completed with greater validity. If the individual demonstrates characteristics or behavior that are generally believed to be incompatible with the demands of police work, the risk in hiring such individuals can be reduced by psychological screening.

Areas of Psychological Screening

The process of psychological screening may be divided into several categories. Each may have several components, and the information from each is considered, in combination with the others, to make a judgment regarding the suitability of the candidate. The evaluation should consist of the following.

Intellectual and Cognitive Functioning Assessment. This part of the evaluation assesses intellectual functioning as measured by various intelligence tests. Basic academic achievement in reading and writing may also be assessed. Perceptual or learning disabilities that could interfere with adequate performance or judgment are an area of particular focus. If deficiencies or deficits that could interfere with performance or judgment are evident, the individual may be found unsuitable.

Personality Assessment. Several measures and techniques designed to measure the emotional status of the individual are employed. The purpose of these methods is to determine the presence of any psychopathology, or any psychological characteristics or qualities that would indicate a high risk of inappropriate or harmful behavior. Scores on tests are analyzed in conjunction with information from other instruments and from a clinical interview. The experience of the clinician with police agencies is essential, especially in making judgments about the emotional suitability of the candidate.

Clinical Interview. While the information from tests and inventories is essential and tends to be more objective than other sources, there is also a need for a more individualized, in-depth method of assessing the candidate. Specific areas of concern can be probed by a professional trained in the identification of emotional and psychological difficulties. Face-to-face observation of the individual's behavior can be a valuable component when the psychologist must make critical decisions. Most psychologists feel that no candidate should be eliminated from consideration for a job based on written psychological tests alone. The clinical interview is a critical step in the screening process.

Form and Basis for Recommendations

On the basis of the assessment process, a recommendation regarding the suitability of the candidate is provided. This can take various forms, but generally provides an indication of risk or fitness. The recommendation is provided to the employing department to assist in a final decision about whether or not to hire a specific candidate. Since the agency must make the final decision regarding employment, the report specifies an opinion as to the degree of risk involved in hiring the individual. It also provides the background and rationale for the decision. Generally, one of three risk levels is specified.

Low Risk. This rating would indicate that there were no significant factors found during the evaluation that would be likely to cause problems or interference with performance as a police officer, and that there were no significant indications of emotional instability at the time of the evaluation. There may be areas mentioned in the report that could be improved upon, or of which the candidate or department should be aware. However, these would not be considered serious enough to interfere significantly with the performance of the officer or to place the public at risk.

Moderate Risk. This rating would indicate that a candidate is judged to have characteristics that might, in fact, interfere with performance or judgment as a police officer. These would be significant enough to place him in a questionable status with regard to his candidacy. In most cases, unless the situation could be remedied and an appropriate intervention made, or unless additional information was found that lessened the risk, the department would be cautioned about hiring the individual.

High Risk. This category would be used when significant factors indicating a high risk are found consistently in the evaluation. These would include a high probability of emotional instability, behavior that might place either the individual candidate or the public at risk, or that would indicate an emotional, perceptual or ability-related problem preventing the candidate from fulfilling important aspects of the job. An individual with this rating would not be recommended for hiring.

Conclusions Regarding Psychological Aspects of Screening

The psychological assessment or screening of candidates for the position of police officer has two primary goals:

1. Screening in applicants with certain traits or characteristics thought to be associated with effective law enforcement.
2. Screening out applicants whose intellectual ability, perceptual ability or emotional status are such that they would represent a significant risk to the public.

The screening-in process is difficult to achieve with any degree of reliability and validity. This is especially true of processes that have tried to establish the relationship between the measures of certain psychological variables and successful law enforcement. At the present time, there appears to be no convincing evidence for the use of psychological instruments to predict long-term successful performance in the field of law enforcement. There are promising efforts being made and research should continue in this important undertaking.

The preferred choice is the use of psychological instruments to identify conditions or problems that impair the performance of police. There is greater consensus on the use of clinical and standardized techniques for identifying those applicants who demonstrate characteristics or conditions that represent a risk to the public. Such an approach has been widely recommended and has frequently been presented as a necessary step in the process of hiring law enforcement personnel.

Legal Aspects of Psychological Screening

In addition to the social responsibility of police agencies to carefully screen applicants, there has been increasing attention given to the issue of legal responsibility. Recent court decisions have held that the police organization can be held negligently responsible for its employees who have not been adequately prepared for their jobs. Police work is generally considered to be one of the more stressful occupations and, consequently, those entering the profession need to be psychologically and emotionally prepared and fit to handle such pressure. This is especially true since many of the police functions directly affect the public safety.

It has been pointed out that under the heading of vicarious liability, the police agency can be held responsible for the inappropriate actions of its employees. Such liability generally falls under two categories which are negligent admission and negligent retention. Negligent admission refers to the acceptance of hiring of individuals who are not fit emotionally or physically for the job. Negligent retention, on the other hand, refers to the retaining of employees by agencies and supervisors who have indications that an employee is not functioning adequately and who are doing nothing to correct the employee's problem. Therefore, it becomes clear that the responsibility for the fitness of police officers falls to a large degree on the agency and its administrators at both the time of hiring and during the individual's employment.

Three things must occur in order to bring an administrator, specifically referring to a chief, into a vicarious liability suit. First, a civilly compensable wrongdoing must have been committed by the police officer. Next, the officer must have been unfit either when hired or must have become unfit in some way following his being hired. Finally, it must be shown that the administrator knew, or should have known, of the officer's unfit condition. A key factor here is the statement "should have known" in reference to the officer's condition. Ignorance of the officer's behavior or problems, or failure to take reasonable action to ensure fitness, do not appear to be valid excuses. Therefore, those with the responsibility for employment or retention of employees can become liable for the wrongdoing of those employees. Such wrongdoing may be defined as wrongful actions, as well as such omissions as failure to perform appropriately.

In an article on the psychological aspects of vicarious liability, J. Steffel and Rossi make similar points. They refer to two deadly sins: negligent appointment and negligent retention. The negligent appointment problem is a component of the staffing function which includes selection, placement and training. If a person is appointed inappropriately, either because proper procedures were not used or an unfit person was hired, the department may be held liable because it acted negligently. If an unfit person causes an injury to a defendant which results in damages, the agency may be held liable. The article refers to the *Monell* case (1978) which held an employer liable for the actions of a negligently hired employee.

Steffel and Rossi refer to negligent retention as the second deadly sin. This occurs when an officer who has exhibited behavior indicating he should not be retained is allowed to continue his responsibilities as a police officer. Both lack of action when problems are known or suspected, or failure to assess an officer's fitness, may be grounds for a finding of negligence. These authors clearly state that the courts tend to include in the definition of negligence the failure of administrators to take reasonable action. In other words, to do nothing with regard to assessing fitness may be considered negligent. They stress that a tremendous price is being paid for "the incompetent people we hire and allow to continue to work in our system."[9]

These two types of negligence can be demonstrated by the findings in two cases. In *Hild* v. *Bruner* (1980), Senior Federal District Judge Whipple commented, "The court is of the opinion that the jury reasonably could have inferred that Newton's (town) failure to conduct some kind of psychological tests of its police officers, at least after 1975 (when according to expert testimony, such testing became widely accepted), constituted gross negligence."[10] Here the town was faulted for failing to take reasonable action to ensure the fitness of officers at the time of hiring them.

In another case, the city of New York was found liable for a shooting by a mentally disturbed police officer (*Bonsignore* v. *City of New York* 1981). In this case the Second Circuit Court of Appeals upheld a jury verdict of $425,000 against New York City for the shooting by an off-duty police officer of his wife. The court said that the jury properly decided that the city was negligent in failing to adopt adequate mechanisms for detecting officers who are mentally or emotionally unfit to carry guns. Even though an early warning system was used, the jury found that it was not effective in that it had failed to identify the officer's problems even though many of the signs were present. The case summary further noted that the officer had not been required to take a psychological examination either at the time of employment or at any time during his career.

Both of these cases suggest that police agencies can be expected to take precautionary steps to prevent negligent appointment and retention. Failing to take steps to identify officers who may not be fit can be sufficient for a finding of negligence. And, those who have encouraged the use of psychological tests to screen out unfit candidates have pointed out that the use of a psychological evaluation is one way to establish a defense in negligence cases resulting from claims of negligent appointment or negligent retention.

R. del Carmen warns that liability extends throughout the chain of command. He defines negligence as doing something "which a reasonably prudent person would not have done, or the failure to do that thing which a reasonably prudent person would have done in like or similar circumstances; it is the failure to exercise that degree of care and prudence that reasonably prudent persons would have exercised in similar circumstances."[11] Therefore, the responsibility falls at various levels from the agency itself to the level of supervisor. It involves failure to train, failure to protect and failure to supervise. The fitness of officers is one of the major factors in this chain of responsibility. While the supervisor may have immediate responsibility for his officers, the hiring and retention of these men are the responsibilities of the agency. The agency and its administrators can be held liable for failure to assure the employment of suitable candiates.

Conclusions

This discussion has attempted to present some of the current thinking with regard to psychological screening of police officers from the points of view of psychologists, law enforcement personnel and legal professionals. There seems to be general consensus on the advantages of implementing some form of psychological screening of applicants from a social, financial and legal perspective. While the defense against negligent hiring and retention is one motivating factor, equally, if not more important, is the social responsibility of protecting the public and the responsibility to assist those officers who are facing serious problems. The possible financial benefits must also be considered.

While the use of psychological assessment for screening in has not been well established presently, the usefulness of such tools for determining the emotional and psychological fitness of police officers and candidates has been more clearly presented by professionals in a variety of settings related to law enforcement. Psychologists have begun to better understand and communicate more effectively with law enforcement professionals, and those in law enforcement have more clearly seen the usefulness of certain psychological tools. Such a relationship is likely to continue and to benefit the development of professional law enforcement.

Endnotes

[1]Robert D. Meier, Richard E. Farmer and David Maxwell "Psychological Screening of Police Candidates: Current Perspectives," *Journal of Police Science and Administration,* October 1987.

[2]President's Commission on Law Enforcement and the Administration of Justice. *Challenge of Crime in a Free Society.* (Washington, D.C.: U.S. GPO, 1967) p. 388.

[3]*National Advisory Commission on Criminal Justice Standards and Goals: Police* (Washington, D.C.: U.S. GPO, 1973) p. 338.

[4]*Ibid.* p. 337.

[5]New York State Senate Commission on Investigations, Taxation, and Government Operations. *Improving Police Management in New York City.* (June 1986) p. 25.

[6]*Ibid.* p. 30.

[7]Knatz, H.F. and Inwald, R.E. "A Process for Screening Out Law Enforcement Candidates Who Might Break Under Stress." *Criminal Justice Journal* 2(4): p. 1.

[8]Dunaway, J.A. "Police Officer Selection in the Medium-Sized Department." The *Police Chief* 47(1) 42.

[9]Steffel, J. and Rossi. "Vicarious Liability: Psychological Aspects of Vicarious Liability." The *Police Chief* 50(3):135.

[10]*Hild* v. *Bruner*, 496 F. Supp. 93 (1980).

[11]del Carmen, R.V. and Carter, D.L. "An Overview of Civil and Criminal Liabilities of Police Officers." The *Police Chief* 52(8):46.

1. The process wherein a candidate for a law enforcement position has an in-depth, individual assessment by a psychologist is known as
   a. *the selection interview.*
   b. *the clinical interview.*
   c. *the screening interview.*
   d. *the oral review board.*

Discussion:
   The prediction of future behavior in a police recruit is extremely difficult. What are some of the major problems in this area?

Chapter 15
Retention of Officers in the Small Agency[1]

The "free exiter" applies to all police personnel who receive training or education at the expense of the police department and leave the department before police and city management have seen a return on their financial investment. More specifically, the free exiter is usually the newly trained police officer who has received basic academy in-service or specialized training, or the police supervisor who receives managerial or executive training.

No police department is exempt from the free exiter problem. Regardless of the excellent benefits that may be built into the department's personnel system, the free exiter problem can occur, causing considerable loss to a department in terms of experience, knowledge and training funds.

The police supervisor or officer becomes a free exiter for at least one of three reasons. First, he may join another department for more money, better benefit packages, promotional opportunities, future career advancements or a combination of all of the above.

Second, the police supervisor or officer may leave the police department in order to gain employment in another police-related agency. The old saying that "the police department is the recruiting ground for state, federal and private organizations" applies quite well here.

Finally, the police supervisor or officer may choose to leave the department and enter into some totally unrelated field of employment (that is, something quite different from his training and educational background).

Career advancement is understandable since many police chiefs themselves have left a department in order to obtain their first command position. Likewise, many police officers have felt the necessity to leave a police department in order to advance their professional careers. However, both supervisors and officers that have obtained their career positions have generally done so after a somewhat lengthy tenure with the police department that trained them.

Today, because police education and training programs are more accessible and abundant to all personnel, many police supervisors and officers are receiving more training and education compared to what previous police personnel have been able to receive. Given this situation, it becomes apparent that the free exiter could potentially (and in many police departments has) become commonplace.

Considering that small agency police chiefs are being asked to do more with less and that most departments will only be able to do so through use of competent, well-trained personnel, the chief must devise an effective retention program with standards indicating a minimal amount of necessary employment that department personnel must adhere to in order to compensate for the cost of their professional training and education.

Training Contracts: A Solution to the Free Exiter Problem

The general philosophy behind police personnel repaying the police department for their training, through either years of service or reimbursement to the department, is relatively new to policing. It was not new, however, to the Law Enforcement Assistance Administration (now referred to as the National Institute of Justice) as a strategy of keeping newly educated officers in the field of policing (at least in terms of what it thought was an adequate amount of service in return for paying the police officer's education).

While training contracts for individual police departments are relatively new and being used at this point in small numbers, they do offer a wide variety of benefits for the police manager, supervisor and officer.

Legality of Training Contracts

A contract is a binding agreement between two or more people to do or not to do some particular thing that is enforceable in a court of law.

A training contract, if used by police managers, can indicate to city management and police personnel a desire to be more responsive and accountable for the financial costs incurred to the department for the training and education of police personnel.

The most important factor to the police manager, and to the validity of the training contract, is its legality. Generally speaking, an agreement is illegal whenever the agreement itself or the performance called for is illegal. Considering that the training contract would be yet another of the many managerial tools that must be used in a fair and nonarbitrary or capricious manner, it would appear to be a legitimate managerial answer to the free exiter problem.

Managerial Advantages and the Retention Program

Given the expensive nature of the training and educational process of police personnel, the training contract offers the best method of securing the police supervisor and officer once the training and/or educational process is completed.

In terms of the advantages to the police chief for utilizing the training contract, the following is offered. It is hoped that once police chiefs become aware of the training contract they will consider their own uniqueness and benefits to be gained from it in addition to those listed.

First, the training contract communicates the expectations of the police department and ultimately those of the police chief. It identifies and eliminates areas that have in the past been vague or undefined in terms of education and training.

Second, it represents an agreement between the department and the personnel as to the sacrifice of employment or reimbursement for department-sponsored training and/or education. Through such an agreement, the training contract provides a medium through which future conflicts may be resolved.

Third, and perhaps most important given the presence of police unions or associations, the training contract provides a legal document that replaces verbal agreements, states the specifications and provides a proactive approach to developing new managerial policy before police unions or associations are able to gain control of another management tool. By specifically setting policy through the training contract, police managers forego the possibility that police unions or associations will dictate policy.

Finally, the training contract can assist in the creation of a retention program. The training contract gives the police department a moderate amount of stability while eventually leading to some form of continuity in the retention of qualified and professional police personnel.

The retention program then provides not only the police manager with some form of security but it also gives police personnel some financial and psychological stability that allows personnel to concentrate more effectively and efficiently on the job.

Although the training contract may never completely resolve the free exiter problem, it will allow the police manager to have more control over the free exiter. The training contract provides the department with the necessary manpower it needs to obtain department objectives. While it is not a panacea for resolving the free exiter problem, it is a viable solution to the problem of training and education without reimbursement to the department.

The following is an example of a training contract.

THIS AGREEMENT made this ____ day of _____, _____ by and between _____ (Employee) and the TOWN OF (The Town), through its Police Department; and

WHEREAS, the Town desires to employ the above named Employee as a police officer and desires to make such employment contingent upon certain conditions; and

WHEREAS, the Town will train and equip the Employee and expend time, money and effort in this regard;

NOW, THEREFORE, in consideration of the mutual promises and covenants hereinafter set forth, the parties agree as follows:

1. The Town agrees to employ, train and equip the above named Employee subject to the terms and conditions set forth herein.

2. The Town will supply the Employee with a copy of the Code of the Town of _____. This contains the Town Charter and statutes which include, but are not limited to, the Town's organizational structure, code of ethics, employee merit system, personnel regulations and procedures, compensation schedule and employee benefits.

3. The Town will supply the Employee with a copy of the Manual of Rules and Regulations of the _____ Police Department (the Department). Its contents set forth: (a) Goals of the Department; (b) Duties of its members; and (c) Rules of Conduct.

4. The Town will supply the Employee with a copy of the Operational Procedure Manual (General Orders) for the _____ Police Department which sets forth procedures, policy and guidelines to be followed in the performance of duty.

5. The Town reserves the right to demote or release any employee for proper cause or for violation of any of the terms of this Agreement and in accordance with the Town's ordinances and policies.

6. The Chief of Police or his designee has the authority to routinely assign and/or transfer all personnel of the Department as deemed necessary for more effective and/or efficient use of such persons. Any person of the Department may be reassigned by location, days and/or hours worked.

7. The Chief of Police will prescribe the equipment provided, the uniforms to be issued and the manner in which they will be utilized by an employee of the Department. The Chief of Police may prohibit any equipment which may not be consistent with Department goals or which will not effectively promote the interests of the Department.

8. The Employee agrees to accept such employment and to perform such duties within his job classification as are deemed necessary by the Chief of Police for the efficient and successful operation of the Police Department.

9. The Employee agrees to familiarize himself with the contents of the above-mentioned publications and he will comply with all policies, procedures, rules and regulations contained in them.

10. The Employee will serve a term of probation of 12 months from the time of graduation from the Police Academy to determine his adaptability to the work of law enforcement. At any time during the probationary period, Employee may be released from employment without appeal for any reason whatsoever.

11. The Employee hereby agrees to remain with the Department for a minimum period of 18 months from the completion of basic training.

12. Inasmuch as the total costs involved in providing Employee with uniforms and equipment are difficult to calculate and allocate with exactitude and damages for breach of this contract agreement are likewise difficult to assess, the Employee agrees to pay (reimburse) the Town of _____ the sum of _____ (amount), not as a penalty, but as agreed upon liquidated damages, in the event the Employee terminates his employment with the Town of _____ Police Department within the first 12 months subsequent to the signing of this contract.

13. Termination by the Town for any reason, or termination by Employee for reasons of poor health or physical or mental incapacity shall not constitute a breach of this Agreement if such is certified by a licensed physician approved by the Town.

14. In the event the Employee is called to active military duty (U.S. Army, Navy, Air Force, Marines, Coast Guard), has his probationary period extended or is granted a leave of absence during the period covered by this Agreement, the period of this Agreement shall be extended by a duration of time equal to the time of military service, extension of the probationary period or leave of absence, whichever is (are) applicable.

15. The Employee agrees to devote full time, attention and efforts to the Department while on duty, and further agrees that he will not engage or be employed, directly or indirectly, in or by any business or entity without the express written consent of the Town.

16. The Employee will maintain habits which will not reflect unfavorably upon the integrity of the Town, the Department, the profession of law enforcement or the Employee.

17. The Employee will endeavor to maintain good health and report any illness or health conditions or incapacity which may affect his job performance, in accordance with the Town's sick leave policy.

18. The Employee shall, upon orders or instructions, attend and participate in the in-service training programs provided by the Department.

19. The Employee of this Department will cooperate and will answer truthfully all questions raised by superior officers. He agrees to take a polygraph test pertaining to any investigation when this is found necessary or desirable as determined by the Department. Failure to cooperate with the responsible official of this Department concerning the above constitutes grounds for dismissal.

20. In the event of breach of this contract, the Employee authorizes the Town to withhold from his salary the wages and/or accrued annual leave, if any, due at time of termination. The Employee agrees that all money withheld shall be forfeited to the Town to be applied to payment of that portion of the liquidated damages included in this contract.

21. Upon termination of employment with the Department, the Employee agrees to relinquish any and all authority of power vested in him as an Employee of the _____ Police Department. Employee agrees to surrender all clothing, equipment, publications, manuals and/or any materials issued to him by the Town. The Employee agrees to authorize reimbursement to the Town the cash value of any articles mentioned above which are not returned upon termination of such employment.

22. If any section, sentence, clause, phrase or portion of this document is, for any reason, held invalid or unconstitutional by any court of competent jurisdiction, such portion shall be deemed a separate, distinct and independent provision and such holding shall not affect the validity of the remaining portions hereof.

23. The waiver of any covenant or conditions by the Town shall not be construed as a waiver of a subsequent breach of the same covenant or condition. The waiver of exercise of any legal right hereunder shall not be construed as a waiver of any other action or right the Town may have pursuant to the terms of this contract.

24. This Agreement shall become effective at 0830 hours on the first day of employment with the Town of _____ Police Department and it shall remain in full force and effect for the duration of employment with the Town.

IN WITNESS WHEREOF, the parties hereto have set their seals and signatures this date.

ATTEST:

_____

_____

Witnesses   TOWN OF _____

BY: _____(SEAL)
                                              Chief of Police

_____

                                              Employee

Endnote

[1]Nick D. Swanstrom, "Resolving the Exiter Problem," *Police Chief*, August 1982.

1. An effective means by which police managers have devised a retention program with standards indicating a minimal amount of necessary employment that departmental personnel must adhere to in order to compensate for the cost of their professional training and education is known as a
   a. *policy statement.*
   b. *training contract.*
   c. *employment incentive.*
   d. *pre-employment issue.*

2. Which of the following elements are important for a training contract to be considered legal?
   a. *The contract must be used in a fair and nonarbitrary or capricious manner.*
   b. *The number of years for the contract cannot exceed the number of months of training provided.*
   c. *The training must be provided by the department and not the state.*
   d. *The officers' salary for the number of years covered by the contract must be stated.*

Chapter 16
Guidelines on In-service Training[1]

While the area of training is the concern of all police departments regardless of size, the small department chief must look at in-service training closely to ensure that it is cost effective and meets his other needs. The chief should begin his analysis by asking the following questions:

Are you getting your money's worth for your training? Does it meet your needs? These and many other related questions should be asked when assessing the impact of in-service training provided for a law enforcement agency.

Have you or your in-service training agency attempted to identify training needs?

It is important that training be oriented to the needs of your officers and the administration of the department. A simple needs assessment will provide appropriate direction and help to ensure that long- and short-term needs are addressed.

Have you assessed the cost effectiveness of the training? Do you see results from present training programs?

Look closely at the availability of local training; it may suit your needs. Of course, not all training needs can—or should—be addressed locally, but the local availability should be seriously considered in evaluating cost effectiveness. There are also times when it is more cost effective to bring the training to you. Don't hesitate to negotiate with training agencies when your needs dictate the training of significant numbers of your officers.

What are the trainers' credentials? Has the training certification system in your state determined the quality of training they offer?

Training programs of every type flourish across the United States. Some are private entrepreneurs just starting out, while others have been in the business for many years. Some are experts, but many are charlatans and opportunists. It is advisable, particularly when going outside your own jurisdiction, to check on the credentials of those offering training to your department. Check on their "track record" based on previous programs, stated goals and objectives, and their professional approach to training. Ask for references and *follow up on them.*

Does the trainer have an ongoing evaluation process in place for the training? If the training is contracted, do you have an adequate means to evaluate the program?

The contractor should provide you with an evaluation of the program. Any quality training program will provide ongoing assessment or evaluation of the product. Be sure to provide the assessment routinely.

Are the goals and objectives clearly stated and followed?

A training program should be a product of its goals and objectives, and should correspond with the advertised claims. It should go without saying that the program's goals and objectives should mesh with your department's training needs and expectations. Officers enrolled in the training should be apprised of these goals and objectives, since they may otherwise be disappointed or frustrated by unmet expectations.

Does the program offer continuity of training within a topical area?

Training should not seem "broken," but should flow logically from one session to another, each building on the other. If officers' evaluations suggest that the program appeared disjointed, rambling or improperly organized, the problem is one of continuity. A lack of continuity may be the result of inadequate experience or expertise, or may be due to a lack of coordination among instructors. The training agency should, of course, be made aware of such problems.

Does the training provide a lasting benefit to your agency?

No training is cost effective unless it has a continuing, positive effect on operations. Did the techniques learned save the department money and/or solve a problem? What can your employees do that they couldn't do before? These changes should be measured on the job.

Do you require your officers to report their assessments of training programs to you?

Every department should have an internal policy of soliciting feedback from its officers as to the quality and appropriateness of the training provided. If the program content is found to be different from what was advertised, inferior in quality or inadequate for your needs, advise the training agency and do not send others to future programs. If the trainers are legitimately interested in providing quality training, they will encourage your comments and will act on them. The more specific your evaluation, the more the trainer can do to improve the product. Indifference to mediocrity breeds more mediocrity.

Of course, the crux of the evaluation process—required before training even begins—is an assessment of the problems that need to be solved. This *starts* with a needs assessment, but continues with problem analysis to determine if a problem is amenable to change through training or whether environmental or reward-system conditions are the real source of the problem. Much money has been spent on training that serves only to exacerbate problems that have nothing to do with skills and knowledge and everything to do with the working environment and what behaviors are being rewarded. Make sure you aren't relying solely on training when other administrative issues are more pertinent.

Providing and participating in a variety of in-service training programs are important to all police agencies. However, the training should be based upon sound needs, and the programs offered should be evaluated on a continuing basis. Training for its own sake may accidentally solve some problems, but planned and evaluated programs provide needed clarification for the chief executive.

The following is a checklist for conducting a training needs analysis in an agency.

Needs Analysis Checklist

A. The Target
1. Who is to be trained?
2. What are their job functions (task analysis results)?
3. Are they from the same department or division, or from a variety of work units?

B. The Instrument
1. Who will have input regarding needs (chief, division director, supervisor, police officer or all/several of above)?
2. What device will be used to assess the needs (questionnaire, interviews, observation, work samples, written test, performance test)?
3. How disruptive of the work environment will this analysis be and how might this be minimized?
4. What is the timeline for this analysis?
5. The Outcome. For each area assessed:
   a. What is the optimum work product desired?
   b. What is the actual work product observed?
   c. Describe the difference between the two.
   d. State, in behavioral terms, an objective or objectives for the work product when the needs are addressed (this may be the optimum work product or a realistic compromise between the optimum and the actual).

6. The Intervention
   a. Is there a skill deficiency? (Could the worker perform optimally if he/she had to? If yes, there is no skill deficiency.)
   b. If there is a skill deficiency, choose a strategy to address this deficiency: offer formal training; informal training or on-the-job training; or provide a job aid, such as a checklist, written instructions, etc.
   c. If not a skill deficiency, determine if
      1) The performance desired is more punishing to the worker than non-performance.
      2) Non-performance is actually rewarded in some way.
      3) The performance actually matters to the worker because there are significant consequences to the level of performance (good and bad).
      4) There are other obstacles to performance beyond the control of the worker.

Endnote

[1]From an article written by the IACP Training Evaluation Subcommittee, "Guidelines on In-Service Training, *Police Chief*, November 86, p. 22.

Review Question - Chapter 16

Discussion:
What are several important considerations to a small police department chief concerning in-service training?

Chapter 17
Career Development

Over seventy years ago, it was recognized that severe police administration problems were caused and perpetuated by ineffective personnel procedures. The future of the police service in America will certainly be determined by the quality of personnel who can be attracted to its ranks. However, the compensation, promotional opportunities and recruitment practices of most police departments are often unequal to the task of obtaining and retaining the desired number of professional personnel.

Spokesmen for the police profession have consistently called for higher standards of police selection, training and career development. Now—with demands for police services steadily increasing, with the police mission becoming increasingly complex—the time has come to answer that call.

Any effective career development program must be based upon the dual imperatives of the individual's interest and the department's needs. The components of the development program consist of training, self development and job progression. Training and self-development opportunities are found both internally and externally, within the department and outside of it.

A very important principle that should be kept in mind when discussing self-development is that it ultimately depends on the individual to act on his own initiative to improve himself. The individual officer cannot wait for someone else to lead him to his career goals. He must initiate individual projects to enhance his knowledge and understanding of the police career field and to increase his competence in areas of special interest.

Many avenues are available for self-development. In almost every area, officers can attend college and/or specialized training courses, read and discuss pertinent books and periodicals, and participate in activities of professional organizations.

Incentive Programs

Many departments are now providing programs of positive incentives and rewards for educational achievements. Adjusting work schedules, granting leave, paying for tuition and the cost of books and supplies and recognizing or requiring educational attainment in the promotional process are some of the ways police departments are encouraging self-development.

The educational philosophy embodied in career development is one which places equal emphasis on formal job training and activities undertaken by career employees on their own initiative. Education and training relating directly to the person's work experience is a major factor influencing his job performance. The ultimate significance of any learning is the way in which it is applied to the job situation. Work experience cannot be isolated from training and self-development.

Obstacles

Several obstacles to effective career development programs have been identified. These are areas of concern for police administrators, as well as for the individual whose career is directly inhibited by them.

1. Restrictive entrance requirements established by civil service agencies often interfere with the establishment of a true police career system. For instance, a residency requirement which only permits hiring persons living within a limited jurisdiction greatly hampers the selection process that would ordinarily be operative at police entrance levels.

2. Low compensation and generally low prestige in the police service deter a large number of persons with potential from entering police service. The same factors often influence many persons who have entered police work to seek other employment in order to gain higher compensation and prestige. These factors are operative throughout the department from the recruit level to management and executive levels.

3. The high regard for seniority as a condition for advancement tends to discourage talented personnel who feel that they can move more quickly than the seniority promotion system permits. Promotion based on seniority is a virtually obsolete practice in private industry, except in a few instances where work rules are strictly governed by labor unions. A seniority requirement alone makes no distinction between the individual who has contented himself with repeating routine tasks and the individual who has deliberately exposed himself to developmental experiences and has prepared himself to handle increased responsibilities. It is not at all unlikely that the latter individual might accumulate more "experience" in two years than another man could in five years of routine repetition.

4. Most departments have no provision for lateral entry or transfer. Lateral entry refers to the hiring of personnel with no prior police experience; lateral transfer to appointment of an individual with special qualifications and experience in the police field. Lateral entry or transfer

permits a department to recruit personnel on an interagency, intercity, or interstate basis, and to recruit personnel from private industry and other professions at comparable levels of compensation and responsibility.

Department Action

Positive action has been taken by some departments to overcome some of these obstacles and improve prospects or career development within the police profession. Civilians have been employed in non-sworn positions to carry out work that does not require the skill of a police officer; cadet programs have been established, and improvements have been made in both recruit training and in-service training; recruitment programs attract college graduates, and financial assistance is provided to officers who want to continue their professional development by earning academic degrees. Many departments have made significant progress toward overcoming specific career development obstacles. Nonetheless, these efforts continue to be essentially local. They are designed to solve the problems of a single department, and they fail to confront the larger problem of needed professionalization of police services.

Some examples of career development skill areas are:

1. Accident Investigation
   a. Hit and Run Investigation
   b. Traffic Accident Analysis
   c. DWI Enforcement
   d. Selective Traffic Enforcement
2. Armorer
3. Breathalyzer Operator
4. CPR/EMT/Shock Trauma/Advanced First Aid
5. Civil and Vicarious Liability
6. Computer/Data Processing
7. Crime Analysis
8. Crime Prevention
   a. Home Security
   b. Business Security
   c. Community Programs
   d. Program Marketing
   e. Neighborhood Watch Program Coordinator
9. Criminal Investigations
   a. Arson
   b. Burglary
   c. Computer Fraud
   d. Drug Enforcement
   e. Forgery
   f. Fraud

g. Homicide
h. Motor Vehicle Theft
i. Narcotics and Dangerous Drugs
j. Robbery
k. Sex Crimes
l. Vice
m. Other
10. Driver Training/Defensive Driving
11. Field Training Officer
12. Foreign Language Skills
13. Hazardous Materials
14. Hostage Negotiations
15. Instructor General
   a. Defensive Tactics
   b. Firearms
   c. Legal
   d. Physical Fitness
   e. Side-handle baton
   f. DWI
   g. New Age Thinking
   h. Defensive Driving
16. Investigative Hypnosis
17. Interviewing and Interrogations
18. Juvenile Law and Procedures
19. Management
   a. Administration skills
   b. Management of:
      (1) Property
      (2) Evidence
      (3) Records
      (4) Purchasing
      (5) Personnel
      (6) Patrol
      (7) Criminal Investigations
      (8) Narcotics/Vice
      (10) Communications
      (11) Fleet Vehicle Operations
   c. Budgeting
   d. Planning
   e. Leadership
   f. Policy Development
20. Media Relations
21. Motor Vehicle Theft Prevention
22. Officer Survival
23. Physical Evidence Collection
   a. Fingerprint
      (1) Classification
      (2) Collection

    b. Photography
    c. Other
24. Physical Fitness Counselors
25. Self-Development
    a. Human Relations
    b. New Age Thinking
    c. Stress Management
    d. Other
26. Special Weapons and Tactics
27. Supervision
    a. Communications
    b. Counseling
    c. Leadership
    d. Motivation
    e. Performance Evaluation
    f. Other
28. Terrorism
29. Video Equipment Operator

It is feasible that even in the smallest agency career development can occur. The chief can establish certain areas in developing proficiency in his officers and acquire the necessary training and development. Even just helping with the tuition cost or granting educational leave to attend college encourages officers to undertake their own career development efforts.

Endnote

[1]IACP *Training Key* #186, "Career Development".

Review Questions - Chapter 17

1. Which of the following is not an obstacle to an effective career development program within a police department?
   a. *The low compensation within the police profession.*
   b. *The high regard for seniority as a condition for advancement.*
   c. *Fair and impartial assessment centers for promotion.*
   d. *Residency requirements for officers.*

Discussion
    What are some steps that can be undertaken in the small police agency to ensure opportunities for career development?

Chapter 18
Personnel Motivation[1]

Unless you have had some experience with it, the task of supervision has probably impressed you as an easy way to make a living. The supervisor gives the orders, while others do the hard work. The apparent comfort, variety of work and privileges of an authoritative position may prompt you to seek the position for yourself. However, this portrays only a part of the total picture. From your first day on the job as a supervisor, you will be confronted with many problems, responsibilities and situations requiring immediate action. Your troubles seem to multiply at an alarming rate, and you may wish for the simple routine of your old position.

The police organization is a dynamic, complex machine, the basic parts of which are people. The department has made policies and developed operational procedures and specific plans even if they are not all in writing. The desired results, however, will be obtained only if the people of your organization are attuned to those policies. A potentially effective department consists of qualified people in the right places in an organizational structure designed to reach set goals. With properly motivated people staffing the organization, satisfactory, if not superior, performance will likely result.

Repeated studies show that two or three capable people spending the same amount of time on a given project will differ in the amount of work accomplished. This difference is due primarily to varying degrees of personal motivation.

Source of Motivation

The power to increase productivity or effectiveness through motivation starts with the supervisor. People are motivated for various reasons, many of which are beyond the control of the supervisor. The supervisor can do little about a subordinate's off-the-job motivational factors and even with regard to numerous on-the-job factors, he must be selective. The supervisor can obtain some measure of results by trying several motivational techniques over a period of time, selecting those that affect the majority of the people under his supervision in a desirable way.[2]

No matter what the supervisor does, some officers will not respond. Others require coddling or some special treatment for which the supervisor does not have time. The supervisor should concentrate on prime motivation factors that in most cases, will help to increase his subordinates' production: personal identification with the organization, work satisfaction, appreciation for accomplishment, communication, and participation.

Personal Identification

People vary widely in their responses and characteristics. A well-timed phrase may stimulate one person to new efforts of achievement may only add to another's egotism. A third may not be able to handle the slightest criticism; therefore, some other device must be used to motiviate him to improve.

No one likes to be known as the "rookie," the "station clerk," or as the "old man." He wants to be known as "Bill Smith," or "Jim Jones;" all people want to be known for their own personal characteristics. Treating people fairly does not mean they are treated as though they are faceless, anonymous machines. When an employee feels his supervisor is interested only in the amount of work he produces, it follows that he is not going to be satisfied with his job for very long, even though he meets the standards that have been set.

The supervisor must be interested in the employees as individuals. If one of his officers is worried about some personal problem, whether or not it is connected with the job situation, it is likely that his effectiveness will be affected before long. While presumptuous inquiry into the private lives of individuals is neither called for nor desired, it is a matter of concern to the supervisor when a maladjustment seriously interferes with the person's job performance. If sincere interest is shown in an individual's problem, he usually will welcome an opportunity to discuss it. Perhaps the supervisor can help him straighten it out, or at least refer him to someone better qualified to assist him. Often, when all the facts are known, it seems amazing that the person is able to carry on as well as he does. The very fact that the supervisor is interested enough to express concern has an excellent effect on the employee.

Developing Work Satisfaction

Every employee should know and understand the mission of his department and his contribution to the fulfillment of that mission. If, for example, an officer under your supervision works as a desk officer, he should be shown why that position is important in assisting other officers in fulfilling their line duties. When he understands the importance of his job, his respect for it and for himself will increase.

In explaining fully the scope and nature of his duties, the lines of organization, responsibility, and authority are made clear to the employee. Some departments note that they have increased employee job satisfaction more by eliminating doubt and confusion in these matters than by any other single step.

An employee who is not doing well in his job usually knows or senses it, and is usually unhappy about it. He is much more likely to quit his job than is an employee who has a feeling of success in what he is doing.

Everyone who is in charge of the work of other people has some responsibility for training them. Determining remaining needs and ways to meet them must be based upon a knowledge of what the training can be expected to accomplish. In certain situations this is easily ascertained on the basis of common sense and reasoning. Training is usually needed whenever

- a new employee joins the department;
- an officer is assigned to a new or different job with which he is not familiar;
- the methods of doing an old job are changed;
- advancement opportunities require new or higher level skills; or
- the mission, the department, or the working relationships are substantially changed.

Motivation is a primary requirement for learning. The person instructed must have a desire to learn the subject; therefore, the supervisor should consult with the personnel involved before framing the training program.

A person who is doing an unfamiliar task usually becomes tired and feels some stress and insecurity toward the work. Perhaps he observes also that his output is far below that of the trained employees. This is especially true when the output can be easily observed. In such cases, the employee will be aware of his shortcomings and will often have a strong incentive to learn because he feels uneasy about his situation. There is much truth in the statement that the best time to learn something is when you feel acutely uncomfortable about not knowing it. Generally, the idea of training is easily sold to new employees. Older employees, however, are less frequently aware of their shortcomings. To the established personnel, the idea of training in the fields of work familiar to them is often ridiculed. It should be made clear to the more experienced employees that they have not attained their highest performance level in attaining certain specified goals. Better trained employees usually have more freedom of action and job security, and are delegated more authority.

If outstanding work is admired by the employee's group, a desire for recognition and admiration will be an important incentive for improvement. Outstanding performance is not always admired by colleagues, and it may even be scorned by them, simply because they suffer by comparison. This attitude necessarily impedes training efforts, and supervisors must be aware of the possibility of a group's placing restrictions on performance. The supervisor should emphasize improvement of the group, as well as that of the individual.

We know employees improve faster when they are kept informed about their progress. It has also been shown praise stimulates the learning process more than criticism. Still, some supervisors have the false notion that it is necessary only for them to correct faults. When employees are told about their accomplishments, faults and shortcomings should also be pointed out; but the wise supervisor uses the "sandwich method," putting the correction between an acknowledgement of good points and approval of progress. The supervisor must also keep in mind the importance of having the right person in the right job. From the standpoint of the employee's job attitudes, it is essential that he be placed in a position for which he is best qualified because

- he will feel more secure in this position;
- the work will be interesting, challenging and satisfying;
- he can best use his skills and talents;
- he knows he can do the work;
- he will have far less fear of a poor work record;
- he can plan for self-improvement and possible promotion; and
- he can become a member of the team and develop sound relationships more quickly.

Selection of the right person is important not only because it enables the supervisor to get the overall job done more effectively, but also because it diminishes the time necessary for training, reduces turnover, improves employee morale and loyalty and even reduces the need for disciplinary action, making supervision easier.

Appreciation for Accomplishment

When any form of work is brushed aside contemptuously by saying, "Well, that's just a basic police job," it is likely that poor performance will result. Work measurement is the basis for applying a prime motivator—appreciation for accomplishment—and supervisors must recognize and reward good performance. Sincere praise from the supervisor makes the employee feel his efforts are noticed and motivates him to earn more of the same. Failure to recognize the basic desire for recognition, to "be someone," accounts for half the maladjustment troubles of people. The very size of many police organizations contributes to the submergence of the individual.

It is fairly easy to spot and reward meritorious performance. The form this reward should take will vary with the circumstances, all the way from a letter of commendation to compensatory time off. On the other hand, supervisors are sometimes concerned because employees who seem most to need praise do not seem to do anything to earn it. This concern stems from a mistaken impression that a person, in order to receive praise, must do something especially outstanding. An employee need not be deprived of praise just because his overall performance is not as good as that of others. If he makes fewer errors this week than last, he has at least earned recognition for what was a real achievement to him.

The opposite of rewarding good performance is criticizing poor performance or conduct. The amount of effort that should be exercised to "salvage an unsatisfactory employee" cannot be determined easily. A good supervisor tries, if possible, to give him an opportunity to improve. Yet, it is not fair to the rest of the department if one employee does not do his share of the work or if his conduct is unacceptable.

There are few supervisory defects more destructive to good order and good work than the failure to deal competently with disciplinary problems. No supervisor can succeed if he lacks firmness in maintaining discipline or requiring good performance.

Most people want to be proud of what they are doing. Within reasonable limits, the more they accomplish, the prouder they are, and the more they like their job. This is so even when they sometimes complain about how hard they work. Conversely, if they are allowed to "get away with murder," to work in a sloppy fashion, they may enjoy temporarily the pleasure of being lazy; eventually, though, they will become discontented. Most employees would rather work in an efficient organization. They are really not happy with a supervisor who does not demand good work, but instead, permits them to perform in a way that tends to erode their own self-respect. If you, as a police officer, cannot respect your own efforts, you can hardly expect others to do so.

Communication and Participation[3]

Communication: If supervisors were suddenly relieved of the many burdensome aspects of their job, one of the most beneficial uses they could make of the time saved would be simply to talk with their subordinates. Effective internal communication is important to any organization. Whenever there is a conflict or lack of understanding among the members of a department, there is usually a failure of communication. A great deal of stress is caused by management's inadvertent failure to explain why certain actions are being taken. Communication goes much beyond the justification for official acts: it is the means of disseminating and receiving information; it conveys the needs and feelings of subordinates to management; and properly handled, it is a valuable tool in stimulating thinking, interest and, ultimately, motivation.

One of the principal causes of the lack of adequate two-way communication is the size itself of many police departments. The majority of well-established channels of communication within most police departments is one-way, from the top down. At roll call, for example, the supervisor may inform the officers about current local conditions, identify some particular problem requiring attention, or point out new orders and procedures. The situation is similar to a lecturer addressing an audience; besides, time is limited to only a few minutes, and thus conditions for two-way communication are entirely unfavorable. Another frequently used procedure is to post memoranda on a bulletin board. If the subject matter is important enough, space may be provided for each man's initials to ensure that all have been advised. Without such procedures, no one can really say if the information has been adequately communicated. And once the officer leaves the station at the beginning of his tour of duty, the opportunity for communication with the department is further limited by the nature of the job in the field.

A supervisor should take the time to talk with each of his officers before roll call, during his tour of duty and after the tour is completed. He should keep them informed about matters that affect them. A sudden announcement of reorganization, work reassignment without explanation leads to a feeling of "What's going to happen next?" This kind of experience indicates ambiguous supervision and does nothing to contribute to increased effort or harmony. People naturally resist change; they fear change when they don't understand the reasons for it. Further, they resent anything that suggests that they are being moved about like pawns on a chessboard. When an officer knows, however, that his supervisor makes it a practice to give adequate warning of changes, as well as the reasons for them, he does not fear or resist them nearly as much.

Participation: One way for the supervisor to instill subordinates' respect for others is to ask their assistance in solving operational problems. In this way, subordinates develop beyond the usual limits of their jobs. This approach to supervision recognizes the importance of the individual and tends to encourage mutual respect. Participation may take many forms.

- Ask people who will use a new procedure or policy for their ideas before it is put into effect.
- Present specific problems at roll call and request suggestions to solve them.
- Implementation of plans suggested by subordinates demonstrates that suggestions are, in fact, given serious consideration.

In brief, this method is employed whenever there is a need to make subordinates feel they share responsibility for the work. It is bad practice, however, for the supervisor to ask for the opinions of his subordinates on a matter about which he has already made up his mind. They will sense his insincerity, and their opinion of him will suffer.

You must keep in mind that whenever you carry the title of supervisor, you become a very important person, especially to those directly under you. Your subordinates probably spend more of their waking time with you than they do with their families. You strongly influence their happiness and their productivity. It is a heavy responsibility. Whatever else you are doing, you must remember you are working with human beings who have individual needs.

Motivation can come only from within the employee. Employee motivation can be the deciding factor in the success of an operation or of the entire department. The supervisor's function is to provide a favorable environment for the development of the employee. If he can lead and assist the employee in the attainment of his goals, the goals of the department will be accomplished as well.

Endnotes

[1]IACP *Training Key* #164, "Motivation."

[2]Leslie Matthies, "The Art of Better Management," The Systemation Letter, No. 127 (Tulsa, Okla: Ross Martin Co.) 1963.

[3]Matthew J. Neary, "Motivating the Foot Patrolman," unpublished Master's Thesis, City College of New York, 1962.

1. A supervisor's main responsibility is to lead people. His success is measured in terms of ability to get his subordinates to perform. Which of the following would best accomplish this purpose?
   a. Always giving employees a lot of praise.
   b. Helping subordinates satisfy their job needs.
   c. Keeping employees informed about current conditions in the chain of command.
   d. Developing a feeling of comradeship with employees.

2. Most people can be motivated to do a better job; however, some persons fail to respond no matter what the supervisor does. The first thing to do with an employee who does not respond to your supervision is
   a. to ignore the man's work habits and performance.
   b. to recommend a transfer to another unit.
   c. to talk with the individual and try to discover his problem.
   d. to consult with other supervisors to determine how they would handle the problem.

3. Job satisfaction is important to employee morale and motivation. Which of the following would not promote job satisfaction?
   a. Increase in pay.
   b. Increased responsibility.
   c. Increase in communication with superiors.
   d. Increase in employee costs of health benefits.

Chapter 19
Chief's Responsibility in Fiscal Management

A police chief executive is not simply a crime fighter or a policeman of special and superior rank. A police chief is also a business manager who should accept full responsibility for fiscal management of his agency. Moreover, he is a fiscal planner, responsible for developing the future expenditure requirements for personnel, equipment, facilities and programs necessary to accomplish the agency's goals and objectives. While he has an obligation to follow all prescribed procedures, he should, where necessary, urge government officials to improve the jurisdiction's fiscal policies and practices, and he should seek to raise the level of his own fiscal management to achieve the goals and objectives he has established. His role in fiscal management should not be passive; it should be active and progressive.

Fiscal Planning, Budgetary Methods and Controls

When the city administrator and the city council begin their task of allocating funds to all departments and units of government for the following fiscal year, the police chief executive will find himself in a highly competitive relationship with other municipal department heads. The council has difficult decisions to make and is concerned with effecting an appropriate allocation of limited resources according to public needs as expressed and demonstrated by various department heads. Such decisions can never be precisely accurate nor entirely acceptable to public constituencies, and the council is subject to many influences.

Carefully developed budgets with adequate justification of all major items, especially on their first appearance in a budget document, are an important responsibility of the police chief executive. In view of typical limitations of revenue that most local governments face today, the police chief executive must be persuasive but objective with administrators and members of council alike. The chief must demonstrate sound judgment in his budget planning in order to gain acceptance of his recommendations.

The budget document, as it leaves the office of the police chief executive, is the position statement on money needed to initiate, maintain or expand programs, functions and activities of the police agency. Although the executive should not prepare the budget unassisted (except in very small police agencies), the responsibility for a sound fiscal document is his.

While the police chief executive may assign fiscal management tasks to subordinates, accountability for all aspects of his agency's fiscal policies, processes and control is his. Within the framework of his jurisdiction's governmental structure, his accountability is judged and his practices reviewed by the jurisdiction's chief executive and, ultimately, by its legislative body.

In some agencies the police chief executive is accountable to the head of the department of which the police agency is merely a division. In other agencies, he may be accountable to a jurisdictional fiscal affairs officer. Likewise, in many agencies his exercise of fiscal responsibility may be reviewed by a higher unit of government—the state, for example. He will not then handle his fiscal affairs in isolation, independent of appropriate controls.

Delegation of Fiscal Management Responsibility

The size of the police agency dictates, at least in part, the level and kind of direct involvement in fiscal management which the police chief executive prescribes for himself. In the very small agencies he handles all details of fiscal management. In medium size and large agencies, he increasingly delegates aspects of fiscal management, but with no diminution of his own ultimate responsibility and accountability.

Like the agency itself, fiscal management is organized to facilitate goal attainment. For this reason, organization for fiscal management needs the same careful planning and implementation as any other function of the agency. If a fiscal affairs unit is established, it should be an integral and interactive unit within the agency, involving the agency in fiscal management affairs of the jurisdiction and working to improve agency policies and processes.

In large agencies where complexity and size of operations do not permit the police chief executive to devote his personal attention to fiscal procedures, fiscal management responsibility should be delegated to a fiscal affairs officer. The fiscal affairs officer should be assigned to the police agency planning organization or, if not, should report directly to the police chief executive.

In agencies too small to justify full-time assignment of employees to the task, the police chief executive should perform the fiscal management function. If the police chief executive lacks technical ability in the accounting process, he should obtain assistance but retain responsibility for annual budget development, maintain liaison with the fiscal officer of the jurisdiction, establish internal expenditure procedures and controls, and keep abreast of current developments in fiscal management research studies.

The maintenance of effective liaison with the fiscal affairs officer of the jurisdiction is of prime importance. In large cities the jurisdictional fiscal officer will be the city administrative officer; in smaller municipalities it will be the city or borough manager. In any case, it is incumbent upon the police agency's fiscal affairs officer to have the communicative skills to present the budgetary needs of the agency as accurately as possible to the jurisdictional fiscal officer. The chief must be a salesman in the sense that he can sell the agency's needs.

The agency fiscal affairs officer or chief should establish and supervise internal expenditure procedures and related program controls. He should develop adequate fiscal controls over the funds available to the agency in order to stay within funding restrictions, to ensure funds are being spent for authorized purposes, to account properly for monies received from the public and to be aware of possible fiscal problems requiring remedial action.

Review Questions - Chapter 19

1. Full responsibility for the fiscal management of the police agency should belong to
   a. the operations division commander.
   b. the town council.
   c. the chief of police.
   d. the mayor or town manager.

2. The position statement on funds needed to initiate, maintain or expand programs, functions and activities of the police agency is known as a
   a. general order.
   b. budget document.
   c. special order.
   d. fiscal responsibility.

Chapter 20
Fiscal Management Procedures

Procedures in fiscal management must support the policies established by the governing body; if they do not, they should be modified or discarded. Fiscal management procedures should be carefully developed to guide agency employees in budget preparations. Every chief should write fiscal procedures and distribute them to management personnel. The fiscal affairs officer of the jurisdiction should be consulted, and procedures should be compatible with those established by the jurisdiction.

Budget Planning and Preparation

Annually, before budget preparation begins, the chief executive of the city usually forwards a budget message to all agency heads. It is written to lay ground rules for budget preparation, establish time frames for the process (often in accordance with state law), explain the general financial condition of the city, detail how certain costs (such as personnel) are to be itemized and set forth requirements for justification. Properly prepared, it is of material assistance to the police chief executive in preparing his own budget message to responsible police agency personnel.

Although budget preparation should be a matter of serious concern throughout the year to police agency personnel, formal budget development usually is scheduled over a period of six to eight months prior to the mandated budget adoption date. Certain budget review and presentation periods are established informally, some may be prescribed by the city council or the city executive, while others are required by state statutes or regulatory bodies or agencies.

Ultimate responsibility for departmental budgets lies with the municipal legislative body: the city council. All departmental budgets are formally presented by the mayor or manager, usually following extensive preliminary discussions. The budget form is prepared so that even at this last point of decision certain modifications can be made. At the final hearing before the council, the mayor or manager may be supported by the police chief executive.

Total Agency Involvement in Budget Planning

Annual budgets should be developed in cooperation with all major organizations within the agency. Commanding officers of the agency's bureaus—patrol, traffic and detectives—must weigh their needs and present budget estimates that include reasonable and economically sound requests.

In police agencies large enough for functional organization (i.e., requiring development of bureaus, divisions, units or offices), budget development should begin at the lowest supervisory level and should be a consolidation of proposed budgets. Sergeants, lieutenants, captains and persons of higher rank in large agencies should be involved and must assume responsibilities in budget development. Thus, in the staff services division of a large agency, the unit commanders of personnel and training, planning and research and others must develop and justify budgets for their operations.

In small agencies, watch or shift commanders should be involved in the budgetary process. Decisions are then made at each level of command as the budget is processed. In very small agencies the chief alone may prepare the final budget. In larger ones with a planning unit, and perhaps even a fiscal officer, the unit or the officer should process recommendations and prepare the final document.

In large agencies the police chief executive's final decisions on controversial programs or items will be influenced by full staff discussion of a tentative final budget.

Police managers often complain that they do not receive the necessary financial support to achieve their objectives. However, those same managers seldom prepare budget requests with written justifications. Or if justifications are written, they are often poorly prepared. Detailed justifications for a budget item should provide the reasons each item is needed.

A police manager who recognizes a problem of needed financial support should prepare a written justification setting forth the need for the added expense and justifying it. If possible, cost-effectiveness should be demonstrated. To identify problems, every police supervisor should inform his superior of the need for additional personnel, equipment or supplies if they are necessary to perform his task successfully . Every major division or bureau head should consolidate proposed unit budgets to form the division or bureau budget. It is essential that every supervisor and every manager participate in determining budget needs, and it may be helpful if participation extends to the lowest level in the hierarchy. Managers should prepare justifications, but details such as projective costs of fringe benefits should be the responsibility of the fiscal affairs officer.

Division or bureau budget requests should be scrutinized by the police chief to assign priorities to items of the agency budget. The fiscal affairs officer should assist in the review by providing assistance to the police chief executive.

Police agencies occasionally initiate new programs and then fail to evaluate them, especially on a basis of cost-effectiveness. A vigorous analysis of programs should be conducted periodically to evaluate program achievements and program costs.

As an exercise in determining priorities, police agencies should construct a budget at 80 percent of the current operating budget. To merely project a 20 percent across-the-board cut may not be the best way to cut costs and would do nothing to establish priorities. Evaluation of programs for this exercise may suggest abandoning, reducing or modifying some activities within the hypothetical reduced budget. When the budget is reworked on a 100 percent basis, the new order of priorities may substantially influence it and provide essential support for top priority functions. It may result in a more efficient and effective police agency.

Fiscal Control

Without adequate control over allocated funds, police agencies could run out of funds needed to carry out their programs. For this reason, in addition to fiscal controls established by municipal controllers, police agencies should develop and adopt well-designed fiscal controls to inform management on the status of the various salary, expense and equipment accounts, and take remedial action, if necessary, to bring these accounts into balance.

Unforeseen situations invariably arise where the need for additional police services cannot be anticipated by prior fiscal planning efforts; therefore, it is essential that interaccount transfers be available to the police chief executive and major element commanders. An example of such a situation may occur from additional funds needed to compensate for overtime expended during natural disasters or civil disturbances.

To provide for such contingencies, various mechanisms of adjustment should be available within the budget system. These options should include transferring funds from a later funding period to the present period, transferring funds from an account that has a savings to one that requires additional funding, and requesting that additional funds be granted for police needs.

Establishing a highly flexible budgetary transfer process, however, increases the need for prompt and critical review of periodically prepared summaries of expenditures, balances and interaccount transfers. These summaries should consist of reports on allotments and encumbrances, and should be viewed promptly by the police chief executive and by the head of each major organizational element within the agency.

By exercising the proper administration of fiscal controls, the police agency fulfills its civic responsibility to provide prudent fiscal management of the taxpayers' money without neglecting the necessary level of police services expected by the community.

Systems Budgeting Experimentation

The concepts and practices of government budgeting have changed in the past few decades. Historically, budgeting has been control-oriented and this is the essence of the line item budget. A new concept of management need resulted in performance-oriented budgeting in the mid-1950s. Another planning-oriented concept subsequently received acceptance: it is the Planning Programming Budgeting System (PPBS).

A systems budgeting process, such as PPBS, may offer advantages to large police agencies. Such systems, however, are not universally applicable. Because of their cost and complexity, they must be studied carefully before complete or even partial adoption. Nevertheless, the police administrator should study and test new budgetary methods. He should use them where it is likely they will help him achieve agency goals better than the methods he has used in the past.

Line item budgeting developed from an obvious need for expenditure accountability—its purpose was control. It remains the most common budget system. In fact, it may be the only practical system in very small jurisdictions, or in large ones when fiscal management talent is lacking.

Line item budgeting is essentially cyclical budgeting. Its basic concern is with the next fiscal year and it is largely based on the current or previous year's budget. It provides great detail on the objects of expenditure and simplifies the comparison of one year's recommendations with the prior year's expenditures. Its use results in discrete additions to particular line items from year to year. It is neither performance- nor program-oriented. Its cyclical nature is both its key advantage and its key disadvantage. It does force—perhaps not too objectively—an annual review of expenditures with reasonable attention to functions, activities and policies.

Line item budgeting also provides varying degrees of control over administrative products and work products, though it has a less effective control over the latter. It is usually effective in requiring budgeting on the basis of organizational units and specific items of expense. Because of its focus on particular aggregate expenditures to perform a service, line item budgeting is classed as one that is input-oriented. On the other hand, there is a danger that it may tend to foreclose long-range planning. It may result in "getting by for another year" without consideration of, or action on, important expenditures and revenue needs of ensuing years.

Other problems confront the user of the line item budget, especially in large jurisdictions. There is no provision, for example, for integrating planning, budgeting and control. Line item budgeting also makes it difficult to relate budgeting to objectives, and expenditures to accomplishments. Objective evaluation of alternative means of gaining prescribed objectives is impractical. It provides neither a sound basis for resource allocation nor a means of measuring the impact of current budget decisions on subsequent budgets. Finally, inherent in line item budgeting is a restriction on administrative flexibility with regard to ongoing affairs; the police chief executive has little freedom to make even nominal changes in expenditure patterns and trends.

While line item budgeting remains common practice, particularly in small cities, it fails to support the concept of budgeting as an on-going process.

Performance budgeting is considered outmoded by some. By others it is considered an extreme form of program budgeting. The performance budget relies on work units and costs per unit as the basis for budgeting and subsequent evaluation of services. It is management-performance oriented. Under performance budgeting, management works with broad appropriations and great flexibility in moving or shifting resources so that they serve program ends. The performance budget is characterized as an input-oriented budget, but less so than the line item budget.

A performance budget, in contrast to one based solely on objects of expenditure, is oriented to major functions and activities to which input (money) is directly related; it anticipates that there will be objective, quantitative measurement of achievement in relation to resources allocated or used in particular functions.

The person or office developing a performance budget for a particular fiscal year will be expected to define appropriately the agency's objectives for the year, the specific activities or programs needed to achieve those objectives and the cost. Pure performance budgeting, as described here, has limited application in police agencies and should be used initially in areas of work where quantification is clearly feasible. Performance budgeting requires careful attention to sound, effective and efficient management records systems, and it depends on sophisticated programs of cost accounting.

Planning programming budgeting systems attempt to join long held concepts and practices of government. PPBS makes it possible to conscientiously select alternative programs designed to accomplish similar ends, and alternative functions and activities to support the program selected. It also assists in assigning priorities to competing activities and in resolving problems arising from apparently conflicting activities. Thus, resources can be allocated on rational bases within integrated systems or among disparate subsystems. Within PPBS, systematic analysis is applied to processes in use to ensure their efficacy and to make adjustments when necessary. Very importantly, PPBS is a multiyear approach to departmental budgeting.

Thoughtful police chief executives, municipal executives and legislators will recognize that the shortcomings are often present in local government budgeting. Often program review for decision-making is frequently concentrated within too short a period. Objectives of the department's programs and activities are often not specified with enough clarity. In many cases future years' costs are not laid systematically enough.

Police agencies that use PPBS also provide other forms of budgeting. Often the jurisdiction's governing body wants to base budgeting decisions on the type of budget to which they are accustomed. Therefore, they may require a line item budget in addition to the PPBS.

Review Questions - Chapter 20

1. A crucial factor for the chief of an agency to include when requesting a budget item is
   a. *the public interest in the item.*
   b. *the written justification for the item.*
   c. *the cost of the item.*
   d. *the local supply of the item.*

2. Annual budgets in police agencies should be developed in cooperation with the following:
   a. *other city departments.*
   b. *community interest groups.*
   c. *all agency components.*
   d. *the chief's office and the city treasurer.*

Chapter 21
Labor Relations Guidelines for Police Administrators[1]

The emergence of unions and collective bargaining has necessitated a redefinition of the police chief's role in the labor relations process. Accommodation to change is crucial to achieve both organizational goals and minimize labor-management conflict in police agencies. However, some chiefs still have not recognized this while many others are uncertain about the kinds of responses needed to make the necessary adjustments in their role. This section has been designed to facilitate change by outlining the various aspects of the police administrator's role in labor relations and providing guidelines for the development of a proactive posture.

Recognition

Once a union has been recognized, the police chief must be prepared to give more time to labor relations generally and to the union in particular. Additionally, if the relationship is to be harmonious, the police chief must work to develop a rapport with employee representatives. George Eastman, in *Municipal Police Administration* states, "This is done by open-handed dealing, with an attitude of acceptance—not by fear, not by tricky dealings, not by trying to get rid of the organization [or its leaders]. The point for the chief to keep in mind is that its [the union's] members are still his employees."

Collective Bargaining

Most police administrators have had difficulty defining their role in the collective bargaining process. There are several reasons for this including the newness of the process itself; the fact that some chiefs have come up through the ranks of and still identify with unions; and the frequent lack of proximity between city hall (generally the hub of collective bargaining activity) and the police department. Actually the role police chiefs should have in the bargaining process is twofold, prebargaining decisionmaking and representation at the bargaining table.

Prior to negotiations, the police chiefs should meet with other public officials such as the mayor or town manager, the council or its representatives and the finance director. With them, he should develop specific offers and counterproposals to be made at the bargaining table.

The police chief's input into prebargaining decision making is imperative in order to inform public officials about the potential impact of city proposals and union demands upon his ability to run the department. For example, many city representatives are not aware of the direct relationship between provisions pertaining to overtime, seniority, accumulation of sick leave and other management rights issued and the capability of a police agency to respond to community needs. Moreover, city representatives have tended to maximize their own interest in "holding the line" on wages by unwisely trading off concessions affecting management rights and departmental operations.

Involvement of police chiefs in prebargaining decision making becomes even more important after the first contract has been negotiated. These administrators can provide valuable feedback regarding the workability of an existing contract which is essential to formulate a viable management position in subsequent negotiations. This feedback provides the rationale for exercising provisions which have had a detrimental effect upon departmental operations and/or labor-management relations and for altering the contract to meet the changing needs of police agencies.

In a small agency, it is suggested that the police chief does not involve himself directly in negotiations. The chief should not act as management spokesman but rather limit his participation to that of an advisor.

Keeping Control

In a study published by IACP the following essential management prerogatives were identified as essential for police chiefs to keep in order to manage their agencies effectively and efficiently and to meet their obligations.

1. The right to plan, direct, and control operations and set departmental policy, goals and objectives.
2. The right to control staffing, schedule work assignments, and set transfer policy.
3. The right to effect disciplinary transfers.
4. The right to select the most qualified officers.
5. The right to deploy a balanced work force.
6. The right to establish work and performance standards.
7. The right to assign officers to needed training.
8. The right to hire, fire, and promote.

9. The right to discipline officers for misconduct.
10. The right to contract for goods and services.

The collective bargaining process does impact on the ability of police executives to meet their obligations as managers. The above listed rights are essential for the proper management of a police department and these management rights must be safeguarded during the bargaining process.

Contract Administration

In a bargaining relationship, contract administration is as important a function as negotiations. The terms and conditions embodied in an agreement are related to the work situation through the process of contract administration. Management has the primary responsibility for initiating policies and programs to implement contract provisions. These policies and programs are especially important in the early stages of unionization and contract development when labor-management conflict is usually greatest. Although this section focuses on contract administration, most of the principles discussed here apply equally well to nonunion agencies in rules and regulations dealing with administrative directives and grievances.

Dissemination of Information. A checklist system must be established for verifying that all personnel in the agency have received a copy of the contract. The police chief should encourage union leaders to meet with their members and explain the contract in detail. Assisted by the personnel director, the police administrator should conduct a similar meeting with his staff and explain expectations regarding implementation of contract terms. Additionally, the chief and supervisors must be made to recognize that *ad hoc* employment practices can be used effectively by the union as a weapon in grievance proceedings. In some cases it may be advisable to supplement these meetings with written memos to ensure consistent application of the contract by all supervisory personnel.

Managerial Training. Some of the key factors to remember with respect to contract administration are:

1. Learning by example is an important aspect of managerial training. Therefore, if administrators are fair in dealing with employees, consistent in their application of contract terms and responsive in delegating authority to administer the contract, these behavioral patterns are likely to be emulated by other management personnel.

2. Police chiefs should work with city officials and outside agencies to provide training for managerial personnel. Ideally, this training should include a mixture of on-site seminars and discussion groups, as well as formal.

Delegation of Responsibility. A considerable administrative effort is frequently required to implement many contract provisions. The provisions subject to this type of administrative action may include leave time, vacations and clothing and cleaning allowances. Depending upon agency size, responsibility for administering these provisions should be delegated to a specific staff member and monitored by the police administrator. Some examples are appropriate to illustrate this point. The contract may require police officers to submit a bona fide receipt to be eligible for reimbursement of clothing and/or cleaning expenses. It then becomes management's responsibility to review these receipts and make disbursements accordingly.

Administrative action is also an integral part of management compliance, especially where the economic terms of a collective bargaining agreement are concerned. For example, fluctuations in the Consumer Price Index must be monitored and corresponding changes made in the rate of compensation to comply with a contract containing a cost-of-living escalator. Similarly, compliance with a longevity provision means that management personnel must continually review seniority lists to determine which employees are eligible for these benefits and make sure they are paid the appropriate amount.

Grievance Handling. Police administrators should make managerial training in grievance handling an integral part of departmental policy. This training should emphasize (1) the interpretation of contract language, past practice and precedent; (2) the importance of documenting the facts as the basis for management's position in grievance proceedings; (3) the desirability of settlement at the lowest possible level as a means of minimizing costs and antagonism between the parties; and (4) skills in responding to grievance, both orally and in writing.

As the last intradepartmental step in the grievance procedure, the police administrator is obligated to evaluate and respond to a grievance within contractually established time limits. Before he accepts this responsibility, however, the police administrator should make sure that management's position has been properly documented. When the rank structure dictates, the chief must also guard against efforts by individual employees or the union to bypass their immediate supervisors and appeal directly to him. Otherwise, the authority of supervisors will be undermined, the net effect of which can be a breakdown in the work relationship.

To the extent that the facts justify, the police chief should support his supervisors in his response to the grievance. If a subordinate has made a mistake, it is often in the best interest of both parties to turn the grievance back to that individual and allow him to rectify it. This tactic can be advantageous in minimizing the potentially ill effects of the mistake for both the manager and the employee or union involved.

Since many grievances tend to be settled intradepartmentally, the police chief should also keep records of the types of issues that have been contested. These records are vital to the police chief's role as a feedback agent in prebargaining decision-making. Based upon the records, he will be able to identify provisions that should be clarified or changed to remove tension from the working relationship.

Working with the Union

Proactive administrators recognize that a mutual interest exists between the labor and management in improving the quality of law enforcement. The shared interest both parties have in law enforcement provides a basis for accommodation and the growth of a working relationship directed towards acheiving the organizational goals of police agencies. Various schemes can be used to bring labor and management together in working towards common goals.

Communications Schemes. Several communications techniques can be used effectively to achieve the goals of police agencies. These are:

1. Informal meetings with union leaders. Especially as a bargaining relationship matures, both police chiefs and union leaders often realize that they can develop a rapport without sacrificing the specific interests they represent. By developing this rapport through informal meetings, both parties find that their ability to anticipate problems and work out solutions before conflict results is greatly enhanced. The success of this particular type of interaction, however, depends very heavily upon the personalities of the individuals involved, the level of communication skills they possess and the security of their position with their respective constituents.

2. Occasional invited appearances at union meetings. The indications are that this type of communication is most successful when the appearance is limited to a discussion of one specific issue. Furthermore, the ability of a police chief to communicate in this type of setting depends very heavily upon his personality rather than on the facts at his disposal. Some of the police chiefs have used appearances at union meetings to stop disruptive rumors and to explain issues which could have resulted in labor-managment conflict without the facts being known. It should be recognized, however, that timing and the receptivity of union members also plays a large role in the effectiveness of this type of communication scheme.

3. Meetings with representatives from the ranks. Some police chiefs have found that periodic round table meetings with rank and file employees have been useful in developing positive labor-management relations. One advantage of these meetings is that they have a cathartic effect on employees by allowing them to voice their gripes and problems. These meetings can also provide valuable information to police administrators regarding deficiencies at the supervisory levels in the agency.

In a collective bargaining environment, prior union approval should be solicited to avoid an unfair labor practice charge. The police chief should also make it clear from the outset that no promises will be made or action taken outside of established departmental channels. To be successful, moreover, employees must not fear reprisal for statements made during the meetings. If these meetings are to be self-sustaining, employee suggestions must be selectively acted upon and the outcomes made visible.

Participatory Management. Participation is one of the most important issues in police labor relations. Employers everywhere are confronted with the challenge of dealing with employees who have attained higher levels of education and who have substantial demands to achieve self-realization and satisfaction in their jobs. Police chiefs should work with union committees in developing new policies. Key areas in which joint labor-management consultation seem to be most successful include uniform changes, officer safety, crime control and job enrichment. Consultation groups are usually set up first, through informal communication between police chiefs and union leaders. Officers are then selected by union leaders to research specific questions and present recommendations to the administrators. Some police chiefs seem to have been successful in enhancing employee satisfaction, involvement and, in some cases, improving productivity through this participatory management technique. The quality of research done by union members is usually high and recommendations are often adopted with little modification.

New police chiefs contemplating establishment of joint consultation schemes should seriously consider the following propositions:

Participation in decisionmaking by the less powerful will change the leadership function of the more powerful; and new structures for leadership, decision making and communication will develop. In the development of new structures, however, participation is in danger of becoming a power struggle between those who stress the need for more participation by employees of the organization and those who emphasize the necessity to preserve the capacity of the organization to function effectively and to survive.

More specifically, many police chiefs have balked at the idea of collective bargaining. However, they are likely to be even more strongly opposed to participatory management which is designed to further extend the area of shared decision-making to include specific aspects of departmental policies.

Experiments with participatory management in both the public and private sectors have shown that employees are usually concerned with specific programs in their personal interest, not with difficult areas of policy making or organizational problems. Furthermore participation is [frequently] promoted primarily by members of the intellectual or academic levels of society. Consequently, these intellectuals often act on the basis of their own motives and abilities without investigating the same factors and preferences of employees who are actually involved in joint consultation. For example, the success of participatory management schemes depends heavily upon the level of expertise and the time available to employees involved in joint decision making. At times, participatory management serves as a good means of removing some issues from the bargaining table.

When collective police bargaining exists in a department, it is essential that both the police chief and the union recognize that a mutual obligation exists to make collective bargaining a viable assist in achieving their responsibilities and objectives of providing better police service to the public.

Endnotes

[1]Adopted from the IACP book, *Critical Issues in Police Labor Relations*, 1977, p. 23.

1. The role which police chiefs in a small agency should have in collective bargaining activity within the department is to

   a. *advise all participants and not involve himself directly in negotiations.*

   b. *have little or no input into process.*

   c. *have total control of process.*

   d. *participate in prebargaining decision making and be represented at bargaining table.*

2. Perhaps the most important way in which a police chief can influence the emergence of unions and collective bargaining is to

   a. *keep lines of communication open.*

   b. *not get involved in process.*

   c. *maintain control of situation.*

   d. *delegate responsibility to a subordinate.*

Chapter 22
Planning[1]

Planning is required on a conscious level even in the smallest agencies. Four fundamental factors point up the need to develop a planning process:[2]

1. To offset uncertainty in change
2. To focus attention on objectives
3. To achieve economical operation
4. To facilitate control

Planning should precede the introduction of any program, system or effort, and it should involve all units and levels of the police organization. Every member of the department should in some way help in determining unit goals and resources, and in finding ways to accomplish needed tasks. Without planning, effective organization, direction and control is impossible. A well conducted planning process results in considerable saving of resources, both material and human.

The Need

Police agencies are continually confronted with the need to cope with change—change created by social and community attitudes, legislation, legal interpretations and administrative decisions. A department must constantly review and clarify its continuing objectives, and at the same time develop methods and procedures to achieve newly defined goals. This is planning.

The most familiar planning occurs on a short-range, day-to-day basis, usually directed toward the solution of some specific problem, and requires very little research and analysis. Short-range planning is necessary in every police organization and serves a definite purpose. However, the planning function should not end there. The kind of planning needed most in modern policing is long-range in nature, designed to develop more effective operations. Planning usually involves much research, analysis and perhaps experimentation.

Objections to Planning

To most people change is uncomfortable; it upsets their normal, daily routine and requires adjustments on their part. There is frequently an attitude of resistance and a desire to perpetuate outmoded or ill-conceived procedures, rather than admit they can be improved. It is easier to police the same beat year after year than to realign boundaries periodically as the need for coverage changes. It is simpler to continue to use the same forms, even if they are inadequate, than to learn to use new ones.

To some, a change in procedure is an admission the former way was wrong, so the suggested change is an implied criticism. Only the "perfect" method, technique or procedure is not subject to improvement. Because change is continuous, planning must be also; few, if any, operations will be performed in the same way every day. However, just because a change results, it does not mean it is for the better. Change without planning often is as bad or worse than no change at all.

Uncertainty about changes creates physical and psychological problems giving rise to more alternatives, and the rightness of any decision becomes less sure. Planning can remove much of the uncertainty and chance in these operations, and if everyone involved understands why, the change can be smoothly implemented.

Planning Mission

The planning function, if it is to be complete, must include the entire management cycle in which research and development play key roles. The planning mission involves five steps:

Plan. Analyze the situation and determine what is to be accomplished. Develop policies and procedures within which the plan will be implemented. Establish measurable goals, the attainment of which will accomplish the plan. Determine and evaluate all alternate courses of action. Develop a plan that will best implement the course of action selected.

Organize. Develop the function required to accomplish the mission. Group-related functions. Define and establish organizational relationships. Assign responsibilities and delegate authority. Select and assign personnel and other resources. Ensure good management through a workable span of control.

Coordinate. Ensure lateral and vertical communication throughout the organization. Establish standard operating procedures and administrative instructions. Coordinate programs and policies to ensure balance among plans and actions. Promote intelligent cooperation and mutual understanding. Encourage acceptance of the organizational objectives, and integrate action toward a common goal.

Direct. Determine the extent of direction necessary, and select methods of communication that will convey, to the pertinent elements of the organization, the action desired. Motivate individuals and units toward the action desired, communicate the requirements and supervise execution.

Control. Determine the type and extent of control necessary. Implement control procedures. Evaluate established procedures. Review and analyze results and take any required corrective action.

Planning Areas

The actual assignment of tasks will depend largely on the number of personnel available. However, there are three areas in which intensive and continued planning is justified and basic.

Management. The chief in a small department must be active in the planning process, although he can involve other personnel. To do this, statements of policies and standardized, understandable procedures as well as definitions of duty, responsibility and authority at every level of the organization are required.

Management planning concerns equipping and preparing the department to do the job, rather than its actual operation as an organized force. All aspects of organization and management of personnel and material, and the procurement and disbursement of funds are mapped out in advance. This includes an organization plan (with definitions of the duties of the component units), budget and procedures for accounting, purchasing and personnel management (recruiting, training, rating, selection for promotion, discipline and welfare).[3]

Management is also responsible for working out cooperative relationships with other governmental departments and community agencies. This has often been referred to as extra-departmental planning.

Operation. The work that the line units must accomplish is analyzed. The nature, time, place, task, etc., is measured in terms of manpower and equipment requirements. Once the desired objectives and procedures for their achievement are defined, the required personnel and equipment are identified and can be assigned to each function.

This operational planning may be accomplished by the police officer working in the concerned area or by a supervisor. This study must include manpower allotment, distribution and operation methods. Actual decisions, however, are a matter of policy and the responsibility of the chief of police, with input from the officer.

Procedures. These plans constitute the "standard operation procedures" of the department and comprise every procedure that has been outlined and officially adopted as the standard method of action to be followed by all members of the department under specific circumstances. Such things as reporting regulations, keeping records, dispatching procedures and procedures for stopping, questioning, searching, handcuffing and transporting persons are all included.[4]

To ensure that no confusion will result, procedural plans must be clearly and concisely stated. Each one must be continuously studied and researched with appropriate modifications when required. These procedures are planned to guide officers in their duties and should be so complete that impulsive and arbitrary decisions by individuals are avoided and cannot be made without deviating from the standard procedure.

Tactical plans for handling parades, demonstrations, sports events and other community activities are prepared as procedure plans.

Steps in Planning

The mechanics of planning can be broken down into several phases, all directed toward achieving the desired results of the organization. If the mechanics of planning are not completely carried out, if one step is omitted or performed in a haphazard manner, problems will develop. There are five basic steps in planning:[5]

Recognizing the Need for the Plan. A need for a plan must be recognized. However, it is not necessary to be confronted with an emergency situation before making plans to handle situations. Projection of possible future needs and contingencies is an intergral part of planning. Critical or tactical problems and conditions should have priority, and then as they are resolved, attention can be given to the long-range view. The need for a plan can be developed from statistical data and information on such things as coming events that may impose unusual burdens, crime variations (increases of robberies during winter months, shoplifting during weekends and holidays) and public events. This need can also be uncovered through inspections. Inspection is not an occasional process; it is continuing, and above all, straightforward. Stealth and deceit have no place in a good inspection technique. Inspections should discover a planning need before there is a breakdown and failure in a procedure. Needs, discovered after a breakdown or failure, reveal that a critical analysis was not made. Warning signs indicative of a need to review and analyze plans and procedures include: the injury of an officer, prisoner escapes, decrease in crime clearance, etc.

Statement of Objective. There will be overall objectives for the entire organization and objectives for the component parts. The statement of objective will outline what is to be accomplished. It must be precise in order to designate the areas in which data is to be gathered and analyzed, and the areas in which details necessary to reach the objective are to be drawn. Here the objective (or often the problem) is isolated and clarified. Steps are taken to assure the analysis concerns the cause, and not a symptom.

Collecting and Analyzing Data. The plan is no better than the information used in its formation. This must be factual and pertinent to the objective. An objective and plan based on complete and accurate information can answer the questions: What? Where? When? Who? How? and Why?

There are several sources that can be drawn upon to provide the necessary data. Usually the first step is a review of the literature in the field. Generally, the subject would not need to have been studied previously by a police agency. There are few problems that a department will experience (especially in areas of personnel, budget, organization, etc.) that have not been handled in other activities. Internal records, reports and documents will provide a basis for predicting operational needs and supplying data for systematic plans.

Most of the original ideas, opinions and suggestions leading to improvements come from individuals directly involved in the area of study. Those who face the problem daily will be able to provide information that is not otherwise obtainable.

Care must be taken to appraise the accuracy of the facts used in planning because decisions made on erroneous facts have a small chance of being correct. After all available facts have been gathered, certain forecasts or assumptions have to be made. It is necesary at times to look ahead to be sure that future operations will not be adversely affected by current decisions. Of course, not all future events can be accurately predicted, but reliable forecasts can frequently be made.[6]

Details of the Plan. At this stage, on the basis of the analysis, it is necessary to decide which of the several and tentative courses of action would be best to outline and implement. The far-reaching effects of the decision must be recognized.

Planning must provide for alternative courses of action. Those that offer the least benefit should be eliminated so that the choices do not become confused by virtue of their number. Alternatives must be carefully evaluated and consideration given to all factors that might affect the future.

Now the plan must determine the course of action to be followed. This involves the decision-making apparatus where one of several plans may be adopted. When a final decision is made, lateral plans must then be drawn-up. For example, in a disaster plan, subplans for fire equipment use, patrol car assignments, hospital emergency room procedures and many other factors must be prepared.

Acceptance. After all of the plans have been detailed, it may be necessary to "sell it" to the people involved in using it. Generally, if the people involved in the new plan *participated* in its development, they can easily adapt to it. The failure to explain to all personnel their part in achieving large organizational objectives will result in their feeling that they are not a part of the system. Officers are expected to contribute toward at least one of the major organizational objectives, and this should be explained in sufficient detail.

Endnotes

[1]IACP *Training Key* #159 "Planning."

[2]Koontz and O'Donnell, *Principles of Management*, (New York: McGraw-Hill, Inc., 1964), pp. 79-80.

[3]*Municipal Police Administration*, (Washington, D.C.: International City Management Association, 1969) p. 214.

[4]Ibid.

[5]O.W. Wilson, *Police Planning*, (Springfield, Illinois: Charles C. Thomas, 1968) pp. 14-17.

[6]Glen D. King et al, *First-line Supervisor's Manual*, (Springfield: Charles C. Thomas , 1970) p. 32.

Review Questions - Chapter 22

1. In order to avoid confusion in plans implementation it is important that a plan
   a. be distributed to agency personnel.
   b. be clear and concise.
   c. be supported by patrol officers.
   d. be cost-effective.

2. In a police organization, the planning mission is to
   a. plan, organize, coordinate, direct and control.
   b. plan, direct and analyze.
   c. plan and incorporate.
   d. plan and implement.

3. The need for police planning is exemplified by which of the following statements?
   a. Failure to plan has hampered the police profession and long range planning is now necessary.
   b. Planning is not as important in small departments because the person who fails to perform can be easily identified.
   c. The police must meet the continuous need to cope with change.
   d. Individual officers must be bound together to achieve effective law enforcement.

Chapter 23
Department-wide Planning[1]

A well-known basic principle of organization is that the effectiveness of the whole is dependent upon that of its several parts. The planning operations of a police department, therefore, can only be as effective as those of its individual members.

The intelligent planning and execution of police operations must be based upon critical estimates of the situation, involving statistical interpretations of records data. Records begin with the line officer. Data compiled from individual reports provide the basis for analyzing crime and determining manpower needs and assignments as well as aiding in budget preparations. Of great importance in crime prevention and control, for instance, is the intelligence upon which administration must rely. This information is derived from organized data in police records.

To further illustrate this point, several planning functions and related line responsibilities are described below.

Distribution of the Patrol Force

The allocation of manpower in a police department is of vital concern, not only to the police executive but also to the city administrator and to the taxpayer, since it directly affects crime, safety, tax rates and services to the people of the community. The quality of law enforcement depends greatly upon the distribution of police personnel, especially patrol officers. Proper staffing and equipping of the patrol force are, therefore, of prime importance.

While the number of officers required to handle the investigation of an offense, accident or incident can be determined, it is more difficult to distribute patrol forces effectively. Complex problems arise when we try to decide how many officers should be assigned to each watch and to each geographic section of the community.

To determine the size of a line division, particularly the patrol force, we must calculate, by time and place, the amount and type of the workload. Demands occur in fairly systematic and predictable patterns over an extended period of time and, by analyzing recorded calls for police service, reasonably accurate predictions of future requirements can be made on the basis of historical experience.

From the workload pattern, we can ascertain the number of patrol beats required for each shift. This number will vary from shift to shift as workloads seldom occur in equal proportions. Similarly, individual beat configurations can be structured so each will have a proportionate share of the workload. Once the beat configurations are established, manpower in sufficient numbers can be assigned. Consideration must also be given to unusual demands for service and to days off, vacations, holidays, training and other activities that detract from an officer's productive time.

Sources of Information

The information used in making these complex planning decisions is furnished by the line officer through his written reports. At some time, most officers have questioned the many details requested on the report forms—"time of call," 'time of report," "area of reporting," etc. All this is vital to the department in determining workload, geographical and time distributions. Accurate reporting is mandatory.

Activity Reports. An activity report is a daily record of the events in which the officer participated in some manner. The form is a running log of all activities, including investigations, assists to other officers, court appearances and "patrol time." It should indicate vehicles used and the mileage, the time assignments are begun and terminated, case reference and numbers and names and addresses of persons interviewed. This document serves a variety of administrative purposes, including use as an aid in determining manpower and vehicle needs, and as a check list of reports due from officers.

Accident Reports. The basic purpose of traffic law enforcement is to obtain voluntary compliance with traffic rules and regulations by motorists and pedestrians. Traffic law enforcement should be applied especially at places and times where accidents occur more frequently. Moreover, enforcement must be directed toward those specific violations that most frequently contribute to accidents. All police records, including accident reports, must be pertinent and complete so they can be periodically summarized and analyzed for the purpose of identifying problems and the best solutions in controlling traffic.

Tactical Planning. Careful review of reports prepared by the officers in the field may lead to the detection of circumstances and features common to a number of cases under investigation. Similarities existing in the areas of modus operandi, physical description and the like may indicate that one individual or group has committed several offenses. Provided with such information, the chief can better coordinate and direct the effort of the department. He may recognize patterns and relationships, formerly overlooked, that should be more fully investigated.

Tactical planning is necessary to the success of temporary, short-term measures designed for specific problems or incidents. These may be critical situations where an overwhelming concentration of striking power is needed at a particular time and place. Those departments in which proper attention is given to special operational planning and execution can meet these crises as they arise without weakening the effectiveness of general police operations.[2]

Armed with all pertinent data from the records concerning police problems, the police department is in a position to launch programs to lower the number of offenses being committed. Efforts may be directed at residence burglaries, car thefts, drug problems, traffic problems or other crimes.

Another example of how records provide information for tactical planning is the modus operandi study. The information in these files comes initially from the details in the line officers' reports. Then the classification of particular groups or types of persons committing crimes is made from analyses of age, race, sex, residence and other characteristics. This is then incorporated in the modus operandi studies.

Field Interview Cards. Field Interview Cards (FICs) are an additional source of valuable information. Items collected from FICs often assist in apprehending suspects or add to material in "known criminal files" by listing companions, automobiles, current employers and the like. The line officer, by providing accurate and complete cards on all persons interviewed during his tour of duty, supports the department's special planning operations.

Planning Programs. Information from reports such as traffic citations, activity logs and arrest reports are probably cross-filed in the following indexes:

1. Name index—names of arrestees, victims, complainants or witnesses are filed in a name index.
2. Crime classification index—a card or slip is filed for each major or selected type of crime by the Uniform Crime Reporting (UCR) classification to assist in UCR preparation, in locating a report when the name cannot be recalled and in questioning suspects. When a case is cleared by arrest, the class index card is pulled and the clearance, name and arrest date noted.
3. Traffic accident classification index—a card or slip is filed for each accident by the classification shown on the monthly form sent to the National Safety Council.
4. Property identification index—a card is made for each item of property worthy of inclusion in a property identification index. All lost, stolen, found, registered and other property status items

are included in the central property identification index. Found and recovered property can then be matched with lost or stolen property.

5. Location index—the card is prepared by location of incident and placed in the file under the street name, in house and/or block number order.

Requests for Police Services

Reports submitted that describe the various services performed assists in planning, analyzing, managing and deploying personnel. These reports reflect all requests for police service—crimes, traffic matters and incidents, regardless of classification—in terms of type, location and time. They are usually provided on a weekly, monthly and annual basis and can be viewed as a master program, serving as a source of information for a number of the programs below.

Selected Offenses. This program is directed toward identifying UCR Part I and other selected offenses in terms of classfication, time and location. This information, issued on a weekly, monthly and annual basis, provides the department with data on current police problems.

Traffic Accidents. This study reflects the time, classification and location of all traffic accidents reported to and investigated by the department. It provides the base for selective traffic enforcement. The information is generated weekly, monthly and annually with cumulative comparisons with previous periods.

Uniform Crime Reporting. This program is designed to keep files and incident reports up to date on any changes, reclassifications and clearances. UCRs are made up directly from this material.

Summary of Arrest Data. Arrests are summarized in terms of classification, time, location and arresting officer. The report is generated weekly, monthly and annually, and ultimately can be correlated with data provided by the analysis of selected offenses. It also serves as an administrative performance record since it reflects individual officer activity.

Traffic Enforcement Performance. This analysis provides information concerning the issuance of citations by time, location, classification, citation number and issuing officer. In addition to the obvious citation control benefits, supervisors can examine the work of each officer and determine whether or not the enforcement effort is properly directed at the specific causes and locations indicated by actual accident experience.

Manpower Distribution. The manpower analysis program is designed to assist the department in distributing personnel, preparing budget reports and projecting future budget requirements. In general, manpower should be concentrated in problem areas—at those locations and during those times shown by experience to present crime or traffic hazards.

Daily Bulletin. When it is practical, many police agencies publish a daily bulletin for the information of the department. Multiple copies can be prepared for distribution to each member. The bulletin is a particularly valuable device to keep patrol officers informed on crimes, wanted persons, stolen automobiles, etc. It also improves roll call procedures by eliminating the need for supervisors to read from lengthy original documents.

Intradepartment Cooperation

Cooperation is necessary if the best use is to be made of resources. Personnel assisting with the planning process must understand the department's goals and direct their efforts toward assisting the line to accomplish these goals. The line personnel, in turn, should understand the various planning functions. This is accomplished in some departments at staff meetings where exchange of thoughts and ideas can take place.

Another way in which the planning staff, and in small departments this is often the chief, and the line units work together in planning is the "pilot study." Pilot studies are a method of collecting data from field experimentation. For example, a department may consider the adoption of new equipment such as a holster or uniform. Certain members of the department will be assigned to use the equipment on a limited basis in order to obtain data for comparison. Pilot studies may also be conducted to examine the effectiveness of new procedures, methods or tactics.

Planning activities deal with change. People tend to resist change when they think of it as merely a different way of doing things. Change may be seen as disrupting the status quo and as a personal threat. If new methods are viewed in this way, they may adversely affect the operating efficiency of police personnel. Therefore, the chief has an obligation to show other members of the department that the planning function is directed toward finding better ways of doing things. When a new procedure is seen as an improvement, people will not cling to the status quo. Rather, they will accept new ideas with enthusiasm. Therefore, good communications is essential throughout the planning process. The sharing of ideas throughout the various stages of planning can help if

1. Personnel realize that the changes are designed to be beneficial, to make work easier, more effective or safer.
2. Personnel have an opportunity to offer suggestions, ideas and comments concerning the aspects of a plan that directly affects them.
3. Personnel are kept informed of the results.
4. Personnel are able to check up on how well they are doing in terms of the change.

Police agencies are confronted with a continuous need to cope with change created by new social problems, community conditions, legislative enactments, legal interpretations and administrative decisions. The police service must continually clarify its goals and objectives, and at the same time develop methods and procedures to achieve these newly defined goals. Without planning, effective direction and control would be impossible, for there would be nothing to direct and nothing to control. Planning must precede the introduction of any program, system or effort.

Implementation. The most important way in which the police officer participates in the planning process is in the actual implementation—putting the plan to work. Many plans directly affect the personnel in the field: a new report form, different arrest and booking procedures or new radio terminology. Before some of these can be effected, the chief will need to provide the officers with in-service training sessions or training at roll call. Although changes in accomplishing a familiar task may seem unnecessary or tend to complicate or increase the workload, officers must be provided the understanding that the changes have been carefully designed for a specific purpose.

An officer who discovers discrepancies in plans or procedures should not hesitate to point them out to his supervisor. Many times the person who works closely with a problem can see errors and solutions much more clearly, and make suggestions that would be welcomed. If an officer believes he has a better solution, he must not keep it to himself. It is his responsibility to share ideas with others in the organization. On the other hand, the officer should not make the assumption that his plan will be accepted; there may be circumstances or other barriers of which he is unaware, and which would prevent implementation of the idea. There must be opportunity for feedback between the officials receiving the idea and the person providing it. It is discouraging for an officer to spend time working on what he thinks is a "great" idea to pass it on and never hear of the idea again. Each person must be informed that his suggestion was received and what action, as well as the reason for the action when appropriate, is being taken.

Good planning results from sound research. Many facts in a broad spectrum of areas must be recorded and examined before any course of action can be taken. It is the line personnel who must furnish a great deal of this factual information.

In the final analysis, the success or failure of any plan rests with the officers who must place the plan into action. The need for change can originate from the patrol officer through his reports, observations, suggestions or personal evaluations of existing programs. Success must also rely on the same factors.

Endnotes

[1]IACP *Training Key* #167 "Department-wide Planning."

[2]V.A. Leonard, "Police Organization and Management," (Brooklyn, NY: The Foundation Press, Inc. 1964), p. 255.

Review Questions - Chapter 23

1. An effective method of keeping departmental members informed of events of interest to all members of the police department is to
   a. *publish a daily bulletin.*
   b. *hold weekly staff meetings.*
   c. *hold daily staff meetings.*
   d. *print a weekly newsletter.*

2. The most important factor from which good planning results is
   a. *cooperation within the agency.*
   b. *sound research.*
   c. *implementation of the plan.*
   d. *direction from the chief.*

3. The intelligence upon which the police administration relies as a tool of management is derived from
   a. *confidential informers.*
   b. *information available in police records.*
   c. *organized and detailed analysis of specific tasks and functions within the department.*
   d. *purposeful and relevant dialogue and communication among staff personnel.*

Chapter 24
Police Chief Survival Skills[1]

Good leadership skills and power skills are essential to survival of a chief of police. Simply stated, leadership pertains to people, organizational purpose, direction, future and managing an enabling work environment where your people believe they and their work are important. Power is associated with leadership and pertains to the desire and capacity to have influence.

Survival is defined as remaining, existing or continuing longer than another. Skill is defined as a developed ability to use one's knowledge effectively. These definitions are most appropriate regarding survival skills and these skills can be *developed* and involve *effective* use of *knowledge.*

Knowledge is different from information. Information is unorganized or unrelated data or facts. There is a lot of it out there. Knowledge is information you can use. But knowledge alone is not sufficient for a chief of police in managing the complexity and diversity of local police affairs. Knowledge must be used effectively. One of the most essential factors relative to police chief survival is the chief's sagacity. Sagacity is a keen discernment of men, motives and means. Sagacity also involves effective use of knowledge.

Sagacity is essential for police chief survival. It is critical for one who has the onerous responsibility of managing local police affairs, often without benefit of civil service or employment contract, and who serves at the pleasure of an administrative or elected official. Under such circumstances, a chief of police must survive while doing the difficult or undesirable which, nonetheless, must be done. So often this difficult or undesirable task involves people problems.

The critical role of the chief of police involves leadership. It also involves power and the capacity and desire to have influence. Leadership skills and power skills do not guarantee police chief survival. However, the stronger these skills, the greater the survival potential.

Power management has significance and considerable relevance for police chief survival. A police chief's management of power and influence is critical in an environment of strong police unions, strong organizational culture, comprehensive collective bargaining laws, grievance-appeal provisions, binding arbitration, labor relations boards, impasse resolution and bureaucratized management above the police chief in the form of comprehensive centralized budget and personnel procedures. Management of power is essential for survival in organizations that have considerable power and influence, namely, police organizations.

Police organizations have traditionally been underled and overmanaged. Leadership transcends the day-to-day, internal management of the organization and focuses on purpose, direction and future. Leaders have a vision for their organization. Leaders get organizations interested in what they are becoming and not what they have been. They have the ability to focus on a specific agenda. They convey an extraordinary commitment that enlists others to that commitment. They direct attention to doing the right things right. There is a significant relationship between leadership and excellence.

Effective leaders lead by values. They are able to instill meaning in the vision and agenda they have for their organization. They enlist others to a cause and inspire them to achieve it. They manage by meaning. They emphasize principles and priorities. They focus on cause instead of effect. They focus on the important. They manage by trust through competence, consistency and credibility. Their credibility depends significantly on their integrity and candor.

Competent leadership involves recognition and nurturing of personal strengths to make others feel significant. It has to do with implementations and maintenance of an enabling work environment where people are dedicated to an agenda. Leadership is essentially a people business in developing others to feel they are important, their work is important, their contribution is important and the result of what they do is important.

Therefore, a police chief executive who is an effective leader spends significant time on people problems. The excellent leader has a highly developed concern for people and their work results. Leading people means getting them to want to do what needs to be done for the organization. This also means providing people something to believe in, namely, organizational values. The effective police leader insists on leading and managing by values.

Police leaders are not paid for their time and labor. They are paid for their discernment and influence. Their discernment and influence involves values. Management by values is better than management by objectives. Our decisions are less difficult when we know what our values are. The greater the divergence between an organization's values and the values of its people, the greater the leadership difficulty. The greater the convergence of an organization's values and the values of its people, the less the leadership difficulty.

Effective police leaders have strong achievement characteristics. They are self-controlled, inner-directed and accept accountability. They are optimistic, have a vision and persist in its realization. They do not avoid persons or issues that must be confronted to reduce or resolve problems. They do what needs to be done even though it involves uncertainty, threat or risk. They do not avoid issues to preserve relationships, and they are not reluctant to confront others in an appropriate manner.

Effective police leaders also have strong people-oriented characteristics that are conducive to interpersonal competence. They are candid, open and honest in providing information and seeking feedback. They are consultative but decisive. They accept people as they are and have a positive regard for others. They listen and understand, without judgment, to get a better perspective. They are sensitive to, but not driven by, feelings. Their relations focus on the present, not the past. They provide assistance, when needed and appropriate, help others grow and develop, and excel at team building.

An exhortation should be made regarding the appropriate role of supervisor, manager and executive insofar as survival is concerned. The police supervisor is that person on the management team who should be the expert regarding job knowledge and skills. This pertains to the methods and techniques that should be applied or used on a daily basis in achieving the mission work of the police organization. The police supervisor is the one who directly interfaces on a daily basis with those who do the hands-on mission work of the organization. The supervisor ensures that the work is done.

The role of managers is generally internal to the daily operation of the police organization. This involves resource management, which is the appropriate distribution and deployment of resources to ensure that the work can be done. Managers ensure that the work can be done. Managers also ensure that supervision occurs at the mission-work level. This is most crucial.

The police chief should give serious and significant attention to the police organization's external concerns and relationships. The real opportunities for organizational progress are outside (not inside) the police organization. This external role involves concern about the direction and future of the organization. He is future-oriented in the sense that he is more concerned with what the organization is becoming than with what it has been. He anticipates the plans for the future. This is also closely associated with direction as it pertains to the organization's future.

The police chief should be aware of the adverse results when members of his management team do not perform their specific roles. If police supervisors do not supervise at the mission-work level of the police organization, the mid-management command officers frequently become involved in supervision. If mid-managers do not manage the internal daily operation of the police organization, then the police chief executive becomes more and more involved in internal management of the organization.

If the police chief doesn't use great portions of his time to give serious and significant attention to the external concerns of the police organization, i.e., pertaining to the enterprise, its future and its direction, someone else will. The someone else will often be someone who has a special interest that is not necessarily in the best interests of the police organization. This could have significant adverse implications in the managing of local police affairs.

One final comment regarding the significance of supervisors adequately or properly supervising. The truth of this comment has become painfully evident for too many police chiefs. When police supervisors do an inadequate job of supervising mission workers or do not accomplish supervisory responsibilities, then mid-management command officers frequently become involved in supervisory responsibilities. This means managers must work extra time because their management responsibilities are not accomplished within 40 hours of work. This often results in a 50- to 55-hour work week.

If mid-management responsibilities are not adequately accomplished by managers, the police chief frequently becomes involved in mid-management responsibilities. This results in his working extra time because his leadership and executive responsbilities are not accomplished within 40 hours of work. This often results in a 60- to 65-hour work week. When this occurs month after month and year after year, there is a long-range submerging effect for the organization. The organization drifts because it isn't receiving the necessary leadership direction and begins to submerge although it manages to stay afloat by crisis management, which focuses more on the urgent than on the important.

With respect to long work weeks with frequent regularity, we should consider the consequences of workaholism relative to police chief survival. There are two physicians in California who, as a result of 25 years' medical practice experience, have identified a descriptive profile of workaholics or what they designate as a Type "A" manager personality.

This descriptive profile identifies personal characteristics that also negatively influence police chief survival. Doctors Rosenman and Friedman describe the Type "A" manager as one who is generally impatient, usually under a sense of urgency and strives to think or do two or more things at the same time. The Type "A" personality involves restlessness, decisiveness and perfectionism. This type of personality experiences a chronic sense of time urgency, a sense of struggle and almost always feels vaguely guilty when attempting to relax. This is workaholism.

Doctors Rosenman and Friedman also identify another profile which they designate as Type "B." Type "B" managers are generally free of all the habits and traits that characterize the Type "A" person. They do not suffer from a sense of time urgency, but they do prioritize and recognize the important. They do not become easily frustrated, angered or impatient. They generally enjoy their work, have a sense of achievement and can relax without guilt.

Both Type "A" and "B" managers can be successful. The Type "A" tends to advance faster careerwise; however, Type "B" tends to advance further. But there is one crucial difference—the Type "A" manager has three times as many health problems as the Type "B," particularly heart attacks.

Doctors Rosenman and Friedman recommend the following to become less of an "A" and more of a "B:"

1. Think one thought at a time.
2. Listen without interrupting.
3. Eat slowly and savor your food.
4. Read books that require concentration.
5. Have a retreat at home where you can be totally alone.
6. Avoid people and events that irritate you.
7. Have a 15-minute period each day when you can completely relax.

Power Skills

Power skills are a means of survival for the chief of police. Power is a reality of organizational dynamics. Power is the capacity and desire to influence others to achieve organizational purposes consistent with predetermined values. The essence of police leadership is the management of power. Management of power (the capacity and desire to have influence) is a critical function in organizations with authority and influence, particularly police organizations.

For effective leaders, the desire and capacity to have influence is more important than the desire for personal achievement or the desire to be liked. Effective police leaders do not use power in a self-serving manner. They do not use their power in an authoritarian, impulsive or exploitive manner. However, they do have an influential presence that focuses on cause, importance, principles and priorities. Their power influence tends to be natural, informal and credible. Their authenticity enhances their influence.

Effective chiefs of police manage power in an authoritative manner. In other words, they exert their authoritative influence for the common good of the organization and its people. Leaders with authoritative power tend to be concerned with fundamental fairness, respectful of the dignity and rights of others, nondefensive and self-confident. They are strongly oriented to self-actualization and achievement. They seek challenge and opportunity and do not excuse incompetence in themselves and others. Therefore, police leaders with strong power skills do not avoid what must be done even though difficult or undesirable. The realities of power and the consequences of its management are most significant for chiefs of police.

Enhancing the Chief's Power

There are three basic skills that enhance the power and influence of a chief of police: decisions, delegation and discipline. Let's first consider decisions.

Decision Making Sytles

The chief of police should be aware of the differences in authoritative, consultative and participative decision-making styles. The authoritative style involves the manager's seeking information but not advice from subordinates for those decisions the manager desires to make himself. The consultative style involves the manager's seeking not only information but also advice from subordinates for those decisions the manager desires to make for himself. The participative style involves the manager's seeking a decision from a group of subordinates with whom he particpates as an equal member, i.e., the manager is committed to the group decision before it is made and is still accountable for the group decision. Obviously, participative decision making (group decision but the manager is still accountable for the decision) should only be used on a selective basis.

If most police managers are honest with themselves, they recognize that they use the authoritative style most frequently. There is nothing wrong with this style when appropriately used, and the manager makes his subordinate aware that he will make the decision. However, problems arise if the chief indicates, when seeking information and/or advice, that the decision is to be made by the subordinate or group of subordinates when actually the chief intends to make the decision himself. If the chief intends to make the decision when seeking information and/or advice, he should clarify his intentions.

One final comment regarding decision making: The chief of police should also be aware of two dimensions of decision making and their effects on others' performance. These two dimensions pertain to quality and acceptance of the decision. Both high quality of the decision and high acceptance of the decision by others are necessary for high performance. If either or both the quality or acceptance by others of the decision are low, performance is poor. If acceptance by others of the decision is necessary, but not obtained, then the decision should not be made because it cannot result in high performance.

Delegation. The second basic skill that enhances the influence of a police chief is delegation. Delegation is the single most important leadership activity that can extend the police chief's sphere of influence and free his time for more effective time management. There are self-assessment instruments to assist in determining delegation effective-ness. There are symptoms and causes for poor delegation. There are rationalizations why not to delegate. There are common reasons why delegation can fail. If delegation is to be effective and enhance the influence of the police chief, it must include an accountability agreement, authority clarification, controls that control insofar as feedback and adjustment and supportive confidence in the subordinate or delegatee. Pre-delegation conferences and post-delegation review discussions are essential for extending the influence of an effective police leader who appropriately delegates.

Discipline. Discipline is the third basic skill that enhances the influence of the police chief. Unfortunately, discipline in a police organization is frequently considered in a punitive or coercive sense. Police managers should recognize there are actually three forms of discipline. These forms include positive discipline, constructive discipline and punitive discipline.

Positive discipline involves prevention and focuses on the question, "Why?" It is an attempt to identify and remove or reduce obstacles to work satisfaction and resolve definitional differences of work goals and what work is worth doing.

Constructive discipline involves correction and focuses on the question, "What?" It focuses on the work setting or work situation with the objective to remove or reduce obstacles to work achievement. The constructive or corrective action is taken against the situation or condition that causes the problem.

Punitive discipline involves coercion and focuses on the question, "Who?" It focuses on the person (not the work situation). The objective of this form of discipline is to change an errant person who has demonstrated that he or she won't properly perform the work even though he or she can. When a person has been properly trained and given the opportunity to accomplish the work but has demonstrated he won't do the work, then the discipline should focus on the person and not the work situation.

Survival Potential

Certain essential considerations can favorably or adversely affect a police chief's survival: survival potential, management by values and the essence of power management as they relate to survival.

Four basic factors determine survival potential. These are self, situation, superiors and subordinates. The essential question addresses the compatibility or incompatibility among the four.

Self pertains to your personal values, lifestyle, leadership style, integrity, credibility, reputation, interpersonal competence, priorities and willingness to take reasonable risks.

Situation pertains to the community and its culture. It includes citizen pressure groups, news media and those events and circumstances over which the chief of police has little or no control. Nonetheless, situation factors have a real influence on a police chief's survival potential. How compatible is self to situation? Such soul searching is not a time for wishful thinking.

Superiors pertains to politicians and the bureaucratized management above the chief of police. They may include one or more of the following: mayor, city council, city manager, assistant city manager or public safety director. With regard to personnel and fiscal matters, it may also include personnel director, civil service board, city attorney and finance director. What are their priorities, practices and preferences? How compatible is self to superiors?

Subordinates pertains to the police organization and its culture. It may include unions and labor agreements. What are their priorities, practices and preferences? How compatible is self to subordinates? Obviously the greater the incompatibility with situation, superiors or subordinates, the less the survival potential.

Management by Values

Now let's focus on some essential considerations regarding management by values as they pertain to survival. Management by values has much more potential for survival than management by objectives. Values determine managerial philosophy, principles and practices. Decision making is less difficult when values are known. Decision making by others in an organization is more effective when there is management by values. The greater the correlation between personal values and organizational mission and goals, the greater the understanding, effectiveness, commitment and success of an organization. The less the correlation between personal values and organizational mission and goals, the greater the confusion, frustration, ineffectiveness and failure of an organization.

Managing local police affairs is ultimately a value issue. Therefore, at a minimum, values should focus on competence, commitment, credibility, collaboration and consistency. These values are essential for a police organization and its people. They are critical for effective leadership. These values enhance adaptive fitness and personal worth. They encourage involvement and creativity. They influence mutual trust and respect. They result in less personnel turnover and greater productivity. They enhance public recognition and support. They encourage fundamental fairness and compassion. They support organizational development and progress.

Managing local police affairs is a diverse and complex process. It involves significant demands on experience and judgment. Its mission and goals reflect constitutional standards and ideals. Police are often the agency of last resort to many citizens. Therefore, managing by values is critical for police leadership.

The distilled essence of organizational competence and excellence is a value issue. It is a reflection of an organization's adaptive fitness to realize potential and work consistently with values its people champion. Fitness is a reflection of organizational health. Organizational fitness is determined by the ability of an organization to translate its values into results.

The Essence of Power Mangement

To summarize the essence of power management and its potential for police chief survival, first, we should recognize that power is a positive quality. We should also recognize that there are two dimensions to having power. One side of power is the capacity and desire to have influence. The other side is staying out of others' control. Some power skills that enhance police chief survival are;

1. Know yourself intimately. There are self-assessment instruments available to enhance self-awareness regarding a variety of factors relevant to leadership and others' perceptions of you.
2. Make sagacious use of information, knowledge and wisdom.
3. Focus your values, principles and priorities.
4. Take reasonable risks.
5. Surround yourself with competent people.
6. Don't abuse your authority.
7. Put your adversities to the best use possible.
8. Take a calm approach to leadership.
9. Live an upright life. Don't give others reason to have disrespect for you.
10. Persist.

Power management is the leadership capacity and desire to influence others to accomplish the organizational mission and goals consistent with predetermined values. Power management also pertains to preservation of the police chief's influence in dealing with circumstances that can limit his authority. These circumstances may involve bureaucratized management and pressure groups. There is another aspect of power management. It has to do with sagacity and survival. It is the sagacious use of influence in such a manner as to enhance survival when doing the difficult or undesirable that nonetheless must be done.

All this requires a values-based leadership style. Values provide influence and guidance. Values-based leadership involves selecting a future direction that is compatible with organizational values and sharing that vision with others. The chief of police enlists support to implement his agenda through his influence.

The chief's leadership role involves providing employees the opportunity and means to contribute toward a direction and future they value. Mutual trust, respect and credibility are the essence of this leadership role.

Effective chiefs of police have the vision and capacity to shape the manner in which their organizations are responsive to their communities. These chiefs have a capacity to influence others to translate organizational purposes and values into results. They also enhance their own survival in the process.

Leadership - A Two Edged Sword[2]

Leadership as a trait for police chiefs has always been acknowledged. The only debate is over whether one is born with it, or if one can learn it. Most of the literature supports the latter theory.

There are many non-threatening aspects of leadership that should be embraced by police chiefs. Creating a vision, setting examples and energizing subordinates will normally not cause any problems. A police chief could probably even be a little dramatic and unpredictable and still survive. Few chiefs have been hurt by creating a climate for growth and enabling staff to develop. Self confidence and a positive attitude are also good. What happens, however, when a chief lets enthusiasm, dedication, and perhaps even professionalism push him or her beyond some vaguely defined point? What happens if a chief of police identifies tradition as the enemy, or actively pursues conflict, or becomes a dramatic risk taker? They seem to work in the private sector, but for police chiefs? Acting with almost as much courage as the first person who ate an oyster, police chiefs have defied tradition by: putting officers in blazers and females on patrol; recruiting blacks so the department could be reflective of the community it serves and doing the same with gays; introducing team policing in the 70's and community policing in the 80's; and many other innovations. What is accepted today was irreverent the first time someone suggested it or much worse implemented it. It was inflammatory to suggest that rookie police officers go through an arrest and booking process in another jurisdiction so they could have a personal understanding of the fear and anxiety that accompanies this process for a first time offender.

Perhaps the safest approach, especially for a new chief, is to be a manager, get the job done and have a better chance for job security. Managers do things right, are practical, avoid conflict and strive for order and efficiency although sometimes at the expense of ideas and innovation. Could it be that those chiefs who are able to hang in there and retire were smart enough to be content with being an excellent manager but only a good leader? Perhaps early on in their careers they learned the price of risk taking so that today they are content with process and structure. Maybe that is the way we have been able to institute the changes that have occurred in police work.

A police leader might challenge and change routine patrol procedures; share his power internally and seek external input; integrate minorities into all ranks; decentralize or even consolidate. Having made one or more of such contributions to their profession, they then retreat. Thus, they are able to survive. Others, however, pursue the holy grail of professionalism at great personal and career expense. Perhaps a leader is able to practice his aggressive pursuit of change until the level of tolerance of the political system is reached. If they are still alive maybe they have not pushed all that hard, or maybe they have a very tolerable, or weak governmental structure. This could well be a type of "Peter's Principle" situation. You are successul and keep your job until you pass the level of tolerance of your political system.

The police field needs leaders who are risk takers and visionaries. When and where to demonstrate these traits might be situational rather than universal. There is a thin line between what a political system tolerates and what it rewards.

Endnotes

[1]From remarks by Willis D. Booth and Donald G. Hanna, Police Chiefs Survival Skills workshop, 94th IACP Conference, Louisville, KY. *The Police Yearbook*, 1988.

[2]From an unpublished article by James P. Morgan, Jr., D. Min., Chief of Police, Goldsboro, N.C.

Answers to Review Questions

Chapter 1
1. c. *Lack of finances is usually the main concern of a micro agency chief.*
2. c. *53%.*

Chapter 2
1. b. *Studies have shown that four significant variables between large metropolitan and small rural police forces are salary, education, training and age.*
2. a. *Knowledge of his community. Rural and small town police are in a better situation to know the citizens whom they serve.*
3. *Rural and small town police tend to live where they work. They are a part of the community both on and off duty.*

Chapter 3
1. *The value system of a police agency becomes the basis for developing plans for change and strategies for delivering police services. The statement of values is the guideline for all other activities and functions within a police agency.*
2. *A value system should include community involvement, crime prevention, preservation of democratic values, resource management, employee input, integrity, professionalism, continuity and consistency of operations.*

Chapter 4
1. b. *Distribution to agency personnel. Goals and objectives must be distributed to all agency personnel.*
2. a. *Community needs. All goals and objectives should be directly responsive to community needs.*

Chapter 5

1. d. *The police chief. The responsibility for all policy development within a police agency rests with the chief of police.*
2. a. *In writing. The most effective method of establishing a policy is by putting the policy in written form.*
3. b. *The civilian employees. Civilian employees often comprise a significant portion of a police organization and are often overlooked in decision-making processes.*

Chapter 6

1. d. *Procedures. Procedures are written directives that describe expected methods of operation within a police organization.*
2. b. *The first line supervisor. The first line supervisor within a police department ensures that written directives are followed by officers.*

Discussion: *A department should have a written directives system in order to hold employees accountable for their actions. Employees must know what is expected of them. Clearly stated written directives provide these standards.*

Chapter 7

1. *The chief of police in an agency can minimize ethical problems resulting from the use of police discretion in a number of ways. The chief must carefully regulate and supervise the department's selective enforcement policies to ensure uniformity. Guidelines in writing regarding the use of discretion should be distributed to all personnel. A high degree of ethical responsibility should be fostered among agency personnel.*
2. *Professional commitments in law enforcement include*
   —dedication to service of others
   —personal commitment to service beyond a normal 8-hour day
   —requiring specialized knowledge and skills
   —governing itself in relation to standard of admission, training and performance
   —having mechanisms to ensure conformance and a disciplinary system to punish deviations
   —forming associations to improve their collective ability to enhance service to others
   —being guided by a code of ethics

Chapter 8

1. b. *The code of silence among police officers. In most cases, police officers do not report unethical or corrrupt activities involving their fellow officers.*
2. a. *Nonfeasance.*
3. c. *Police corruption is similar to corruption in other segments of society. It is a serious problem with no easy solutions.*
4. d. *An internal affairs unit only supplements the efforts of line officers and supervisors in keeping a corruption-free department.*

Chapter 9

1. b. *Departmental attitude. A department that condones corruption in any form will encounter serious problems related to the honesty of its officers.*
2. c. *Training. Training in the area of corruption has been superficial in most police agencies.*
3. d. *A gratuity that is acceptable under certain circumstances. Acceptance of a meal or cup of coffee is not in itself an act of corruption. The circumstances surrounding the offer are the determining factors.*

Chapter 10

1. b. *The state law.*
2. b. *Written directives. Officers cannot be disciplined for action that has not been officially prohibited.*
3. c. *Signing a petition without reference to official position is fully within the law.*
4. a. *Police administrators, police officers and the community. These three groups have the strongest influence on police conduct within a jurisdiction.*

Chapter 11

1. c. *The first line supervisor. The first line supervisor within a police department ensures that written directives are followed by officers.*
2. b. *The supervisor must inform command personnel. When a supervisor carries out disciplinary action, command personnel are not always notified.*
3. a. *Required to submit to a polygraph even for departmental purposes.*

Chapter 12

1. c. *The proper selection of police officers. A police department is only as effective as the people in it.*
2. d. *The purpose of the officer selection process is to find the candidate with specific, desirable personnel and professional qualities that would make a positive contribution to the department.*

Chapter 13

1. c. *Assessment Center. The assessment center-type selection procedure is being utilized in many law enforcement agencies for police officer selection and promotion.*

Discussion: *The use of written hypothetical case scenarios during the applicant process enables the evaluator to judge responses in regards to writing skills, grammar, thought organization, the application of common sense in problem solving and content.*

Chapter 14

1. b. *The clinical interview is an in-depth assessment of an applicant for a law enforcement position by a psychologist.*

Discussion: *The major problems are as follows:*
1. *Since there are between 15,000-20,000 police agencies in the United States, a wide diversity in size and type of department exists. In addition, the nature, demands and needs of communities vary tremendously. Therefore, criteria in the form of definitions of effective performance also vary widely.*
2. *Because of the differences noted above, there is a wide variation in police tasks and responsibilities, making standardization of requirements impossible.*
3. *There is little consensus of the "ideal" police officer with regard to behavior and traits. Often the same positive results are obtained in many different ways, by very different kinds of individuals.*
4. *Finally, it is reasonable to expect changes in the nature and make-up of the police workforce over a period of time. It appears that the present work force is more highly educated than was true earlier. It is also clear that the tasks of police officers are becoming more technical, legalistic and socially demanding. Continuous changes can be expected in this field.*

Chapter 15

1. b. *Training contract. The use of a training contract is an effective means police managers have devised to retain personnel subsequent to their professional training.*
2. b. *The contract must be used in a fair and nonarbitrary or uncapricious manner.*

Chapter 16

Several important considerations for a small police department chief to make in regards to in-service training are
1. *Training needs. A needs assessment will provide direcction and ensure that long and short-term needs are addressed.*
2. *Cost effectiveness of training. You need to get the most for your money. It may be more cost effective to bring training to you.*
3. *Credentials of trainers. Check "track records" of training programs and references.*
4. *Training evaluation on continued basis. Constant planning and evaluation of training in all areas of the police department.*

Chapter 17

1. c. *Fair and impartial assessment centers for promotion.*
Discussion: *Some steps that can be taken in the small police agency to ensure opportunities for career development are*
—*providing incentives and rewards for educational achievements*
—*granting leave, paying for tuition and recognizing or requiring educational advancement for promotion purposes.*

Chapter 18

1. b. *Helping subordinates satisfy their job needs. The supervisor who can help satisfy subordinates job needs will receive the best results.*
2. c. *To talk with the individual and try to discover his problem.*
3. d. *Increase in employee cost of health benefits.*

Chapter 19

1. c. *The chief of police. The chief of police is responsible for the fiscal management of the police agency.*
2. b. *Budget document.*

Chapter 20

1. b. *The written justification for the item. The addition of written justification for an expense will enhance approval of budget items.*
2. c. *All agency components. Every component within a police agency should be utilized in budget development.*

Chapter 21

1. a. *Advise all participants and not involve himself directly in negotiations.*
2. a. *Keep lines of communications open. When lines of communications are kept open, agreements can be reached.*

Chapter 22

1. b. *Be clear and concise. Plans need to be clear and concise in order to be implemented with success.*
2. a. *Plan, organize, coordinate, direct and control. The planning mission, if it is to be complete, must include all of the listed steps.*
3. a. *Failure to plan has hampered the police profession and long-range planning is now necessary.*

Chapter 23

1. a. *Publish a daily bulletin. The issuance of a daily bulletin is the most effective method of distributing information to departmental employees.*
2. b. *Sound research. Sound research is the basis for successful results in planning.*
3. b. *The information available in police records is the management tool utilized by administrators.*

Subject Index